READY
FOR
SCHOOL?

WHAT EVERY PRESCHOOLER SHOULD KNOW

MARGE EBERTS
AND
PEGGY GISLER

ᴫ Meadowbrook Press

Distributed by Simon & Schuster
New York

Library of Congress Cataloging-in-Publication Data

Eberts, Marjorie.
    Ready for school?: what every preschooler should know/
    Marge Eberts and Peggy Gisler.
    p. cm.
    ISBN 0-88166-146-5. — ISBN 0-671-73387-7
    1. Readiness for school. 2. Preschool children. I. Gisler, Peggy.
    II. Title.
    LB1132.E23 1991
    372.21—dc20   90-23384
                                                              CIP

ISBN: 0-88166-146-5

Editor: Kerstin Gorham
Art Director: Anne Marie Hoppe
Production Manager: JoAnn Krueger
Cover Design: Jennifer L. Nelson

Simon & Schuster Ordering #: 0-671-73387-7

Published by Meadowbrook Press, 18318 Minnetonka Boulevard,
Deephaven, MN 55391.

BOOK TRADE DISTRIBUTION by Simon & Schuster, a division of Simon
& Schuster, Inc., 1230 Avenue of the Americas, New York,
NY, 10020.

91 92 93 94 5 4 3 2 1

Printed in the United States of America

DEDICATION

To all parents who are diligently preparing their children for school, especially Carolyn and Ken Brody.

Contents

Chapter One

THE PARENTS' ROLE IN EDUCATION

Today's kindergarten is not the kindergarten you remember. Think back instead to when you were in first grade; what you learned then may well be what your child will be expected to learn in kindergarten now. The current nationwide push for academic excellence is rapidly shoving the typical first-grade curriculum back into kindergarten. The kindergarten you remember that let children spend their time finger painting, learning how to share, hanging on monkey bars, and snacking on milk and cookies is rapidly disappearing. Pencils and workbooks are replacing crayons and building blocks. Kindergarten has become so academic that many children now fail this first year in school. More than ever before, it is essential that children be ready for school. That requires parental help.

Frightened by the horror stories of kindergarten dropouts and armed with the best of intentions, you may already have started your child on a program designed to ensure academic excellence from her* first day of school. The good news is you *can* prepare your child for the academic challenges of school. The bad news is that, if you are like most parents, you are going about this important task in the wrong way.

The Workbook and Flashcard Approach

Unfortunately, most parents assume they can give their children a head start in school by concentrating on reading and math. Parents give their preschoolers worksheets and workbooks to complete. They teach them phonics and how to count to 100. Some parents are so enthusiastic about giving their children an early academic advantage at school that they begin teaching reading and math to their two-year-olds. You have probably visited homes of such zealous parents and seen the names of objects plastered on chairs, tables, and beds. You may also have seen parents and toddlers earnestly working together on flashcards with dots or numbers on them.

---

*To avoid sexism, we have alternated using female and male pronouns by chapter.

Too much, too soon

While some children may truly enjoy an early excursion into the academic world, many find it boring or frustrating. Most young children just aren't ready to sit down and concentrate on academic work and are quickly turned off by workbooks and flashcards. Don't try to turn your child into a scholar before she is ready. There is absolutely no evidence that formal instruction at an early age has any lasting academic advantage. It may even do some harm. Pushy parents force-feeding academics to their preschoolers are causing a record number of cases of kindergarten burnout.

Questionable results

Are parents' well-meaning efforts actually teaching children to read or understand numbers? Not necessarily. A child who knows enough phonics to sound out words may not have the slightest idea of their meaning. And a preschooler who can count to fifty may not be able to look at a stack of five objects and tell you how many items it contains. Being able to count like a robot does not show that a child understands numbers.

Limited success

When parents concentrate on stuffing their preschooler's mind with reading and math, they may be pleased with the results when the child first enters school. She may be an academic star in kindergarten. However, by the first or second grade this early advantage usually disappears as her classmates catch on to reading and math. Some children will, of course, begin school as academic superstars and continue to shine throughout their years in school. But for most children, a jump-start in reading and math doesn't last.

What Teachers Expect

Here's a surprise: despite what many parents believe, kindergarten teachers don't consider parental help in developing reading and math skills as important as work in other areas, such as developing language and thinking skills. The following list shows how kindergarten teachers who participated in a recent study ranked the most important areas in which parents could help prepare their children for kindergarten.

Preparation Areas	Rank
Ranked from most important to least important	
Comprehension of the Spoken Word	1
Thinking: Attention Span and Problem Solving	2
Fine Motor Skills (small muscles)	3
Social Development	4
Self-Help Skills	4*
Emotional Development	5
Speaking Skills	6
Prereading Activities	6*
Understanding Numbers	7
Gross Motor Skills (large muscles)	8

Source: Kimberly Harris and L. Knudson Lindauer, "Parental and Teacher Priorities for Kindergarten Preparation " *Child Study Journal* 18 (1988): 66.

*Tie

On the first day of school, teachers want to see children who are ready and eager to learn. They want children to walk into the classroom with the wide variety of skills and experiences they need to handle the challenges of today's kindergartens, not with heads stuffed full of words and numbers.

General expectations

Schools expect children to have some basic skills when they come to kindergarten and usually provide checklists of these skills. Studying such a list well before your child enters kindergarten can guide you in preparing her for school. Most lists suggest that she should be able to do the following:

- handle all her personal needs, such as going to the bathroom or putting on a coat

- play harmoniously with other children, share toys and games, and respect the property of others

- handle conflict situations

- make simple choices

- speak clearly enough to be understood

- express her own needs and wants

- follow rules and understand the need for them
- know and follow basic safety rules
- follow simple directions
- be happy away from home

Academic expectations

Rather than expecting children to be able to read and do math, schools want children who are ready to learn these skills. Most school checklists emphasize that the child who is well prepared for the academic side of school should be able to accomplish the following tasks most of the time:

- tell her right hand from her left
- have a basic understanding of how to use crayons, paints, paste, and clay
- draw rather than scribble
- speak in complete sentences, avoiding baby talk
- name common objects correctly
- tell or retell a story
- work independently for at least five minutes
- listen to a story for five to ten minutes
- listen to a rhyme and hear similarities and differences
- copy simple shapes
- bounce and catch a ball, showing the hand-eye coordination necessary for reading and math
- recognize similarities and differences in the sizes, shapes, and colors of objects
- follow a series of three directions

Parents Have an Important Role

Research by the U.S. Department of Education shows that parents are their children's first and most influential teachers. In other words, the bulk of the important task of preparing children for school falls on the parents' shoulders.

Fortunately, the task of preparing children for school is not nearly as complicated or impossible as most parents believe. It is certainly not necessary to set up an at-home classroom with workbooks, worksheets, and flashcards as so many parents are doing nowadays. However, parents do need to know something about how children learn and how they can foster this learning process.

How Young Children Learn

Young children don't learn like older children and adults. Their intellectual growth is connected to and dependent on their social, physical, and emotional development. In fact, they can't help learning. Much of what they learn about the world comes from the hands-on experience they get while playing. That is the way they learn that ice and snow are cold, discover that wood floats but coins sink, and figure out how shadows are made. That is also the way they learn to get along with other people.

A child's play may seem frivolous and disorganized to you, but it teaches the child what she needs to know. Each bit of learning is a building block for future learning. The infant learns a bright ball can be grasped, the toddler learns the ball can be thrown, and the young child learns the ball can be bounced.

How to help children learn

Children will learn without help from their parents. However, they will learn far more if parents encourage and guide their learning. Here are some ways that you can help set the stage for your child to learn through play:

- See that she has an adequate variety of playthings appropriate for her age. A two-year-old needs big blocks, not a fifty-piece puzzle.

- Make sure that she has playthings, such as boxes and dress-up clothes, that stimulate imaginative play.

- Give her the opportunity to learn as much as she can about the world. Take her to zoos, offices, factories, farms, and stores. Let her walk in the rain. Have her pet a goat.

5

- Give her the opportunity to play with other children.

- Make sure she engages in both indoor and outdoor activities and has chances to play alone, with family, and with friends.

Every child has her own learning clock

Parents understand that children will learn to crawl or walk when they are ready. The same principle applies to the skills children need for school. A two-year-old is not developmentally ready to pick up a pencil and draw a recognizable picture, but a five-year-old probably is. Parents need to remember that children mature at different rates and that a child may be advanced in developing certain skills and slow in developing others.

Observe your child carefully and guard against pushing her to acquire skills before she is ready. This can be difficult when a friend's child is toilet-trained, counting to 100, reading stories, and tying her shoes, and your child has not yet acquired these skills. However, pressuring a child to learn a skill too early may make it even harder for her to learn it later on.

To find out more about children's individual readiness timetables, read a good book on child development, such as one of the following:

- New York Hospital–Cornell Medical Center with Mark Rubinstein, M.D. *The Growing Years.* New York: Facts on File, 1989.

- Tom and Nancy Biracree. *The Parents' Book of Facts.* New York: Simon & Schuster, 1986.

- Fitzhugh Dodson and Ann Alexander. *Your Child: Birth to Age Six.* New York: Simon & Schuster, 1986.

How to Use This Book

Each of the next ten chapters describes a set of skills that children should learn before starting school. The skills are organized in order of importance, based on the list of preparation areas ranked as important by kindergarten teachers (see page 3). We explain why these skills are necessary and include a checklist that you can use to determine whether your child has mastered them. Because children change so rapidly, you should reevaluate your child according to the checklists at frequent intervals. Skill levels can rapidly shift from "cannot accomplish" to "can accomplish easily." We also discuss how children learn different skills and at what stage they will most likely be ready to learn them. Finally, we describe many activities you can use to help your child develop and practice the skills needed for kindergarten.

Both the skills checklists and the activities are divided by age group (Birth to 15 months, By 2½ years, By 5 years) so you can see at a glance what skills your child is expected to have by the time she reaches each age as well as which activities are appropriate to help her acquire these skills. You do not have to limit yourself to using just the activities listed under a child's particular age group. Older children will frequently enjoy doing activites that are listed for younger children, and some younger children may be ready to do more advanced activities.

Remember, each child develops at her own rate. Be sure to choose activities that your child is ready to handle. Don't expect your child to master all of the skills mentioned in each chapter or be disappointed or worried if she doesn't. Failure to master every skill is not likely to be a sign of developmental difficulties or future learning disabilities.

Above All Else

Remember that young children love to learn, and that kindergarten teachers want children to walk into their classrooms eager to learn. Don't kill this eagerness by forcing academics on your child before she is ready. Instead, use the activities recommended in the chapters that follow to expand your child's range of experiences and whet her appetite for learning.

Chapter Two

UNDERSTANDING WORDS

Children begin developing their listening skills long before they are born. While in the womb, they hear digestive noises, heartbeats, and blood rushing through vessels. Their listening skills become so sharp they can tell the difference between their mother's voice and a stranger's. Parents need to keep that sound stimulation going after birth in order for their children to enter school with a good understanding of the spoken word.

On the first day of kindergarten children don't need to understand the language of the Pledge of Allegiance or the Declaration of Independence. But they do need to understand what is said in *Cinderella* and *Little Red Riding Hood*. And they certainly should know what to do when their teacher says, "Color the pumpkin orange" or "Hang up your coat." From kindergarten through college, much of what children learn in school depends on their understanding of the spoken word.

What Children Need to Learn

Today's society demands that children understand thousands of words when they enter kindergarten. So they must develop good listening skills. Listening is more than hearing—it involves learning basic sounds, words, phrases, sentences, and the relationship between objects and their use.

Teachers rank understanding of the spoken word as the number one skill area in which parents should help their children prepare for kindergarten. Use the checklist on pages 10–11 to see how well your child is doing in this area.

How Children Learn to Understand What They Hear

Children are born aware of the sounds around them, and some are quick to attach meaning to individual sounds. When it comes to understanding words, children may have an idea of what a word means after hearing it just once or twice. But it may take them years to learn its full meaning. Say "ball" to a young child, and he may think the word stands for his own favorite blue ball. Or he may think "ball" stands for anything round, such as an apple, an orange, or his brother's head. After a while, he will learn that balls come in a variety of sizes, shapes, and textures. But he won't fully understand the word until he knows the difference between tennis balls, golf balls, rubber balls, and all the other kinds of balls he sees. How much children learn about a word depends on the variety of experiences they have with the word. This is an area where parents can help their children.

Children learn quickly

All children acquire vocabulary at an awesome rate, learning new words almost every day after they are a year old. Prior to one year, however, their ability to understand words is quite limited. Even at nine months a child will only understand about three words. As he grows, the number of words a child understands increases in the following way: a one-year-old understands approximately 12 words; an eighteen-month-old, 100 words; a two-year-old, 300 words; a three-year-old, 1,000 words; and a five-year-old, 8,000 to 12,000 words. Notice the vast jump in language development between ages three and five years.

Learning to understand what sounds and words mean fundamentally changes a child's world. At around three months a child usually attaches meaning to sound, but it is not until six months that he begins to understand a few words and their meanings. Once a child understands "no," for example, he understands that he can't do everything he wants to do. Suddenly, he realizes that his world has limitations. Similarly, understanding "night-night" and "bye-bye" help a child know what to expect. Every sound and word that a child learns makes the world a more comfortable place.

Watch for Signs of Problems

Most children understand the spoken word when they are ready to do so. But this won't happen unless they are able to hear the words. Watch for the following signs, which may indicate the existence of a hearing problem:

- frequent colds
- repeated ear infections

Checklist of expected listening skills

	can easily accomplish	can accomplish with difficulty	cannot accomplish
Birth to 15 months			
Reacts differently to loud and soft sounds			
Looks to see where sounds come from			
Responds to human voices			
Knows the difference between angry and happy			
Identifies different speakers			
Likes to listen to self babble or talk			
Knows the sounds that favorite toys make			
Imitates sounds			
Recognizes own name			
Understands names of familiar people & objects			
Begins to respond to commands			
Understands more words than can actually say			
Associates sounds with objects (drums, rattles)			
Understands "no"			
Enjoys listening to poems and stories			
By 2½ years			
Likes to be read to			
Has favorite storybooks			
Listens to short stories			
Recognizes the words for common objects			
Recognizes the names of people			
Identifies body parts			
Understands the position words *on, under, in*			
Understands simple questions			
Understands simple commands			
Listens for the meanings of words, not just sounds			
Listens to adult conversations			
Repeats sounds, words, and phrases			

	can easily accomplish	can accomplish with difficulty	cannot accomplish
By 5 years			
Appreciates stories, poems, and music			
Listens to stories without interruption			
Recalls story facts			
Retells a simple story in sequence			
Tells the meaning of words heard in a story			
Repeats simple nursery rhymes			
Follows simple two- and three-step commands			
Understands and follows rules			
Recognizes common sounds (animals, cars, running water)			
Distinguishes between loud and soft sounds			
Identifies beginning sounds of words			
Hears the differences between similar sounds			
Identifies rhyming sounds			
Copies simple rhythmic patterns (clap clap — clap clap)			
Imitates common sounds (dog, siren, horn)			
Hears soft whispers and understands the words			
Identifies unfamiliar words and asks their meaning			
Tells the meaning of simple words			
Understands the position words *in front of, behind, toward*			
Understands most adult sentences			
Repeats eight- to ten-word sentences			
Repeats a series of five numbers			
Plays games such as Simon Says			

- failure to identify the location of sounds
- listening to television, radio, or records at a very high volume
- garbled or indistinct speech

A moderate hearing loss is not as severe a problem for older children or adults because of their previous experience with words. For a child who is just learning to understand language, even a minor hearing loss can be a significant obstacle to learning the spoken word. See a doctor if you suspect your child may have a hearing problem.

Creating a Learning Environment

Children don't have to be taught to understand the spoken word. But the level of their understanding depends directly on how language is used in their home. There is a time and an age when baby talk is appropriate (see page 69). However, baby talk should not be a staple of the language your child hears by the time he is three. It makes a difference whether a preschool child hears, "I made a boo-boo" or "I made a mistake." Children develop their language skills best by being exposed to quality language. All the hours you spend talking to your preschoolers, repeating nursery rhymes, reading stories, and singing songs will pay off when your child enters school.

Acquainting your baby with sounds

It's a noisy, noisy world. But don't drown your baby in sounds and expect him to immediately recognize the difference between a barking dog, a vacuum cleaner, and a whistling kettle. Instead, introduce your baby to just one sound at a time. Then he will come to understand that dogs bark, vacuum cleaners roar, and kettles whistle. And talk to your baby, as he will be the most attentive to speech sounds.

Talking to your baby

Most parents automatically know how to talk to their baby and what to talk about. Check this list of suggested activities to make sure that you make good use of your talking time with your baby:

- Tell your baby the names of objects that are part of your daily routine. This helps the baby learn the names of familiar things such as body parts, clothing, and household items.

- Use action words to describe to your baby what you are doing as you scrub, fold, sweep, stir, and read.

- Describe to your baby what he is doing. Tell him that he is banging on a pot or drinking milk. Tell him that he is crawling on the floor or bouncing on your knee.

- Use descriptive words such as *big, blue, round, soft,* and *pretty* to describe toys and other objects to your baby.

- Tell your baby where things are by using position words such as *up, under, behind, in,* and *out.*

Talking to your young child

As your child grows older, conversation plays an important role in helping him understand the spoken word. Just talking, however, is not enough. Speech must be accurate and descriptive. Children don't increase their vocabulary when everything and everybody is called "this thing" or "that person." They need to learn precise words for objects and people. To develop your child's knowledge of words, get into the habit of asking him such questions as, "What shape is the frying pan?" or "Where do we buy potatoes?" You must also answer all those "why" questions. You are your child's personal dictionary and encyclopedia.

A cautionary note: Be careful not to confuse your child by using words far beyond his understanding. Don't say, "Propel the spheroid to your pater." Say, "Throw the ball to your dad." Remember, your child learns from what you say.

Using toys

Most children pick up the greatest part of their understanding of the spoken word in their homes. This environment can be expanded by playing with toys. Almost any toy gives a child the opportunity to learn the meaning of new words. When parents aren't around, sound-producing toys such as record players, tape recorders, and talking toys are good substitutes.

Beware of the TV

Surveys show that children spend approximately twenty-four hours a week watching television. Unfortunately, television does not offer the interaction that young children need to expand their understanding of the spoken word. It also encourages children to get in the habit of paying only brief attention to what is going on. On the other hand, television enlarges children's vocabularies by showing them things such as silos, skyscrapers, zebras, oil wells, and airports. Use television with care.

Activities for You and Your Child

From the moment you bring your baby home, there are many fun activities that you can do together to enhance his understanding of the spoken word. If an activity seems difficult or isn't enjoyable for the child, don't force him to continue it. Find a more appropriate activity instead.

From birth to 15 months

Locating sounds. Have your child listen to unusual sounds such as bells, chimes, noisemakers, and music boxes. Repeat the sounds in different locations. Then vary the loudness of the sounds.

Sharing picture books. Choose picture books that have simple illustrations and then talk to your child about what is on the pages. Use books that have pictures of familiar things in the child's world. Do not expect your child to look at books for long at first; over time his attention span will increase.

Singing songs and reciting rhymes. Introduce your child to simple songs and rhymes. The child will learn about similar sounds, and Mother Goose rhymes will teach him new words. For example, he will learn *mittens* from "The Three Little Kittens" and *fetch* from "Jack and Jill."

Playing homemade musical instruments. Provide your child with two pot lids or a pot and a spoon. Now he has cymbals or a drum to accompany a lively tune on a record or tape.

Clapping to rhymes. Say the familiar "Pat-a-Cake" rhyme to your child while going through the clapping motion (for directions see page 35). Help your child learn to clap. After a while you and your child can clap out the rhyme as you say it, which teaches him to coordinate actions with words.

Learning to follow directions. Ask your child to hand you an object that he can recognize by name, such as a sock, a teddy bear, a ball, or a book. When the child hands the object to you, thank him and mention the name of the object.

From 15 months to 2½ years

Locating body parts. Give your child frequent opportunites to show recognition of the names of body parts. Ask a question such as "Where is your mouth?" Guide your child's hand to the part you name until he can do it independently.

Recognizing family members. Pull out the family photo album and ask your child to point to the picture of Aunt Marcia, Uncle Luis, or Grandpa Jake. This helps the child learn to relate names to faces.

Making picture books. Cut pictures of common objects from magazines. Your child can help you select the pictures. Assemble the pictures into a book and go through it with your child. Let him name the objects he knows. Name the rest of the objects for him. Remember, young children do not immediately associate an object with its picture.

Identifying sounds. Tell your child what you hear, and then ask him if he can hear it. Be sure to mention who or what is making the noise. For example, while on a walk you can say, "I hear a bird chirping; can you hear the bird?" You are developing the child's ability to listen for specific sounds.

Finding objects. Place three similar objects on a table, and ask your child to hand one of them to you. The child practices identifying objects and following simple directions.

Answering yes or no. Give your child lots of practice in answering questions. Play the Are You game with your child by asking, "Are you a tree?" "Are you a bee?" "Are you Michael?" Then play the Is It game by holding up a ball and asking, "Is it a baby?" "Is it a bottle?" "Is it a ball?"

Talking over the day. Each evening, tell your child a story about what he has done during the day. Don't forget to include any accomplishments, such as using a fork or learning to jump. Talking over the day lets your child listen to adult conversation and reviews the events of the day in sequence. At times, you may wish to record one of your conversations for your child to listen to the next day.

Playing the Echo Game. Stand across a room from your child. Make a sound and have him echo the same sound back to you. You could roar like a lion, bark like a dog, clap your hands, or slap your thighs. Make this game easy or difficult to match your child's ability. Add a sequence of sounds such as barking twice or clapping your hands three times to make the game more difficult. This game helps your child become a more careful listener.

Supplying sound effects. Read or tell a story to your child. Pause whenever sound effects are needed and let your child supply them. A story might go like this: One day the family went on a trip. Dad honked the horn (pause for sound) and the dog began to bark (pause for sound). Supplying sound effects helps children listen attentively and recognize sounds made by familiar objects.

Reading stories. Read to your child every day. It will accelerate your child's understanding of the spoken word.

From 2½ to 5 years

Recognizing common sounds. Have your child cover his eyes and try to guess what common household noises you are making. You might run water, rattle pots and pans, vacuum, or bounce a ball. An easier way to do this is to tape common household sounds: doorbells ringing, clocks ticking, computer-keyboards clicking, and cars starting. Be sure there is space between the sounds and that each sound is played long enough for your child to recognize it. As your child gets older, make the activity more difficult by using sounds such as kettles whistling, popcorn popping, and hair dryers blowing.

Recognizing rhyming sounds. Introduce rhyming sounds through rhymes and stories such as *The Cat in the Hat* by Dr. Seuss. Next, chant some rhyming words with your child (*hat, cat,* and *that*) so he becomes more comfortable with the rhyming concept. Then say a group of words and have your child identify the word that doesn't rhyme with the others. Make the nonrhyming word quite different at first:

> hat — cat — that — banana
> jam — ham — bowl — Pam
> hill — pill — fill — tree

Copying rhythmic patterns. Clap your hands and ask your child to clap with you. Say "clap" as you both clap. Try clapping different patterns.

Children also enjoy clapping to songs such as "Row, Row, Row, Your Boat," "Twinkle, Twinkle, Little Star," and "Old McDonald." Sing, hum, or play these songs, and your child can clap the beat. Clapping activities sharpen your child's listening skills.

Row, Row, Row Your Boat

Row, row, row your boat
Gently down the stream,
Merrily, merrily, merrily, merrily
Life is but a dream.

Twinkle, Twinkle, Little Star

Twinkle, twinkle, little star
How I wonder what you are!
Up above the world so high,
Like a diamond in the sky.
Twinkle, twinkle, little star
How I wonder what you are!

Old McDonald

Old McDonald had a farm, E-I-E-I-O!
And on this farm he had a _____, (Name an animal.)
E-I-E-I-O!
With a _____ , _____ , here (Make sound of chosen animal.)
And a _____ , _____ , there.
Here a _____ , there a _____ ,
Everywhere a _____ , _____ .
Old McDonald had a farm,
E-I-E-I-O! (Repeat song substituting different animals and their sounds.)

Following directions. Play Simon Says with your child. In this game, the child follows commands that begin with "Simon Says." Any commands that do not begin with those words should not be followed. Start with Simon asking the child to follow one-step commands. Then go to two-step commands. Some children may be able to follow commands with even more steps. Use simple commands such as these:

Simon says touch your nose. (one step)
Simon Says touch your nose, then stick out your tongue. (two steps)

Add position words such as *in front of* and *in back of* to make your commands more complex and to teach directions.

Repeating sentences. Play Copycat with your child. Say a simple, short sentence and challenge him to repeat it. Start with three words in a sentence and build up to eight- and ten-word sentences. Keep

17

this game fun. Don't ever let it frustrate your child. The activity may be more enjoyable if the sentences are about family members.

Comparing sounds. Take turns with your child in finding loud and soft sounds. If you find a loud sound (a blaring television), the child has to find a soft sound (a purring cat). You can also name or play taped sounds and have your child tell whether it is loud or soft. Expand this activity by finding long and short sounds (moooooooo and woof) or high- and low-pitched sounds (shriek and growl) for the child to compare.

Telling the meaning of words. While reading a familiar story to your child, stop and ask him the meaning of a word. He can point to the object in an illustration or explain what the word means. Try words such as *forest* and *porridge* in *Goldilocks and the Three Bears* or *slipper, ball, coach, pumpkin,* and *prince* in *Cinderella.*

Recalling stories. You and your child can take turns retelling familiar stories. You should begin the story and let your child tell what happens next. Then you and the child alternate telling the story. Don't insist on total recall. Read the story after retelling it to reinforce the correct order of events.

Above All Else

Remember, kindergarten teachers are looking for children who understand the spoken word. Talk to your child. If you fill his days with listening experiences, he will have a larger vocabulary, speak in longer sentences, and have a longer attention span. There is one other significant advantage: children who are good listeners usually become good readers by third grade.

Chapter Three

MAKING SENSE OF THE WORLD

Almost everything children do shows they are thinking. Watch babies feed themselves. After much trial and error, they learn how to use a spoon. Toddlers push the right button and the television set turns on, indicating they have some understanding of cause and effect. You don't have to hear children counting or saying the alphabet to know they are thinking.

Thinking is a skill that is used for every task in school. The first grader painting a picture debates whether the sky should be gray or blue, the fifth grader decides how to arrange information in an outline, and the high-school student predicts the outcome of an experiment. Through thinking, children use information, acquired at home and school, to make sense of the world.

Failure to acquire efficient thinking skills is devastating. Children can't easily memorize poems, important dates, or speeches without good memory skills. If children can't recognize likenesses and differences, they will not be able to classify words as nouns or verbs, a task introduced in first grade. And without problem-solving skills, doing math homework becomes a nightmare.

What Children Need to Learn

Essential to intellectual growth is a willingness to try again and again. Children usually can't snap beads together on the first try, but they probably will on the tenth or hundredth. It is the same with building towers of blocks or riding a bicycle. Finally succeeding at a task teaches children a valuable lesson: they can be successful by refusing to give up. Think of how important this habit is in school, where children are faced with the difficulty of learning to read, write, multiply, and memorize.

Perseverance needs to be learned before children start school, or they may despair if they don't immediately succeed with a task. If you compare the pleasure of completing a puzzle with the pain of learning the multiplication tables, it is easy to see why children acquire persistence through play more easily than through schoolwork. Parents can help children develop this habit by praising their efforts and by not demanding immediate success in achieving goals.

Don't expect your child to think as you do. She won't be capable of complex thinking until she is an adolescent. Use the checklist on pages 22–23 to see which thinking skills your child has acquired.

How Children Learn Thinking Skills

Children from all walks of life develop their thinking skills at about the same time and in the same way. Since early in this century, much of what we know about how children think has come from the work of Jean Piaget, a Swiss psychologist. According to Piaget, children go through four stages of mental development, with different abilities in each stage.

Piaget compares children's thinking to that of scientists solving problems. Both take information and fit it into their existing way of thinking. If necessary, they adapt their thinking to the new information. Children's thinking skills grow because of the interaction between existing ways of thinking and new experiences. For example, a young child might call a bald man a clown because both have bald heads. When the child discovers that clowns also wear funny costumes and try to make people laugh, she learns the difference between bald men and clowns.

Stage one: from birth to about 2 years

In stage one, children acquire a basic knowledge of objects by using their senses. They cannot understand what an object is without having seen, touched, heard, tasted, or smelled it.

For the first month of their lives, children just use reflexes, grasping what is put in their hands and sucking what is put in their mouths. Then from one to four months, they are concerned with repeating pleasurable activities like thumb sucking. Most of their actions are focused on their own bodies. Between four and eight months, they finally become interested in the outside world and try to make things happen, such as hit a ball to make it move. When they are approaching one year, children begin to combine actions to get what they want. They will knock away a pillow to get a toy. Between twelve and eighteen months, children become explorers and look for new ways to do things with objects—a toy hammer isn't used just to pound pegs in a board but to pound almost everything in reach. By about age two, children will begin to think about what they are going to do. They will study a shape before trying to put it in the proper spot on a simple puzzle.

A major concept that children learn during stage one is that objects continue to exist whether or not they are seen. Show an infant a rattle and it exists. Hide the rattle, and it no longer exists as far as the infant is concerned. Children learn gradually that objects exist apart from themselves. By two years, they are interested in playing hide-and-seek games to search for missing objects.

Stage two: from about 2 to 7 years

Children in stage two still haven't made complete sense of how the world works. They know that objects continue to exist when they can't be seen. Early in this stage, however, they don't understand changes in appearance. A three-year-old may think that a boy has become a girl if he puts on a dress. A six-year-old knows this is a ridiculous idea.

Although children in this stage can use symbols, most of their thinking is still based on appearances. If an equal amount of milk is poured into two identical glasses, five-, six-, and seven-year-old children readily agree that both glasses have the same amount. But pour the contents of one of the glasses into a taller, narrower glass, and only the seven-year-old will be certain the glasses contain the same amount. Younger children don't take into account both height and width. For them, more height means more milk.

Stage three: from about 7 to 11 years

Children in stage three know that the amount of milk in a glass isn't more because it has been poured from a wide glass into a tall, narrow one. They now are capable of what Piaget calls "mental operations." Whereas they formerly had to manipulate objects physically, now they can mentally manipulate symbols that stand for objects. They are experts at classifying objects into groups and are ready to learn basic reading and math skills because they can follow rules and apply them.

Checklist of expected thinking skills

	can easily accomplish	can accomplish with difficulty	cannot accomplish
Birth to 15 months			
Reaches and grasps objects intentionally			
Recognizes objects and people			
Is aware of basic body parts			
Uses all five senses to gain information			
Is aware that certain events follow other events (crying brings parent)			
Performs an action to see the effect (drops object on the floor for someone to pick up)			
Imitates play of others			
By 2½ years			
Learns and expects routine			
Sees similarities and differences in objects and people			
Groups similar objects on the basis of one characteristic			
Relies on senses to gain information			
Shows some control of the environment (turns off faucets, shuts off lights)			
Understands that events can be sequenced			
Recalls recent events			
Expects absent people or objects to reappear at appropriate time or place			
Begins to solve problems and make decisions			

	can easily accomplish	can accomplish with difficulty	cannot accomplish
By 5 years			
Recognizes similarities and differences in shapes, patterns, and figures			
Copies simple shapes (square, circle, triangle)			
Identifies missing parts in pictures			
Maintains attention on adult-directed tasks for short periods of time			
Maintains attention on own tasks for longer periods of time			
Practices to gain mastery of tasks			
Gets information by observing and asking questions			
Begins to link past and present information			
Begins to develop simple memory strategies			
Begins to recognize differences between the real world and fantasy			
Realizes actions have both a cause and effect			
Makes simple generalizations			
Groups objects on the basis of one or more characteristics			
Tells what happened first, second, and third			
Shows understanding of general times of day (morning, noon, night)			
Knows colors			

Stage four: from about 11 years

At about eleven or twelve years, when so many body changes are occurring in children, their thinking also changes dramatically. Now they can think abstractly. They can imagine what it would be like if people had eyes in the back of their heads. They can problem solve and form theories. In short, they are beginning to think as adults do.

Creating a Learning Environment

Piaget's ideas help parents understand how their children's thinking skills develop and let parents know what to expect of their children at different ages, as well as what not to expect. Remember these points from Piaget's research:

1. The stage of mental development that children are in places definite limitations on what and how they learn.

2. Preschool children learn best from concrete experiences.

3. Children must make sense of the world themselves. For example, you can't just tell them that people and animals are different; they must figure this out.

To create a learning environment that will help your child make sense of the world, provide a wealth of materials that can be touched and handled. Then help the child see the world as an orderly place. Establish a rhythm to the day by having certain activities regularly occur after others. And have specific places to store the child's toys and other belongings.

A cautionary note: Since children learn through their senses, be sure that all toys and objects they explore are safe for them to handle.

Activities for You and Your Child

You don't have to teach your child how to think. It will occur naturally, like crawling and talking. However, you can plan activities that will promote intellectual growth. Just make sure the activities are within your child's capabilities. Take the lead from the child. See what activities interest her. Then give her plenty of practice time to master an activity.

From birth to 15 months

Tracking objects. Choose a brightly colored object and move it slowly so that your child can practice following it visually. Remember to adjust the object's distance to the child's visual capabilities. Children's ability to see improves rapidly from legal blindness at birth to approximately 20/100 at about four months.

Reaching and touching. Provide your child with interesting objects to grasp or crawl toward. Make sure that the objects are a size she can handle. Do not overwhelm your child with too many objects, and be sure that favorite familiar objects are available along with new ones.

Exploring responsive toys. As your child becomes more coordinated and mobile, choose objects for more active play. Give your child balls to roll, bells to ring, boxes to open, and sponges to squeeze. After she explores a new object, demonstrate some additional things that can be done with it. This increases the child's interest in exploring its play possibilities.

Playing Peek-a-Boo. Partly hide a six- or eight-month-old baby's favorite toy under a cloth or blanket. Your baby will search for the toy. As she becomes older, hide more and more of the toy until she is able to find a completely hidden toy. Your child will learn that objects exist when they can't be seen.

Learning names for body parts. Touch your child's nose, chin, toe, or some other body part as you recite the word in a nursery rhyme, such as:

>Eye winker, (Touch her eyes.)
>Nose smeller, (Touch her nose.)
>Mouth eater, (Touch her mouth.)
>Chin chopper, (Touch her chin.)
>Guzzlewopper. (Give her a hug.)

From 15 months to 2½ years

Pretending. Play grocery store, take imaginary trips to Grandmother's house, or pretend to be a bus driver with your child. This type of imaginary play will move your child beyond simple awareness and exploration of objects and provide her with a greater understanding of how the world works.

Finding similar objects. Find pairs of objects such as spoons, barrettes, shoes, socks, and cups. Place one of each object in a bag and the others in front of your child. Have your child draw one object from the bag and match it to its mate.

Classifying objects. Give your child practice in grouping objects sharing similar characteristics by using everyday activities. She can sort socks by color or find apples in the refrigerator.

Exploring textures. To develop discrimination in the sense of touch, walk around your home with your child and encourage her to explore the texture of objects such as sponges, furniture, and rugs. Your child needs this experience because most toys are made of smooth plastic or wood.

Investigating smells. Expose your child to odors not usually found in a home. Let the child smell recently turned earth, fresh sawdust, or pine needles.

Recognizing basic tastes. Help your child distinguish between the four basic tastes (sweet, sour, bitter, and salty) by calling attention to these tastes in both familiar and new foods.

From 2½ to 5 years

Playing the Color Game. Look around a room and say to your child, "I see something and the color of it is (name a color)." The child asks questions to guess the object. ("Is it the cookie jar?" "Is it the chair?") As your child becomes older, the selection of objects can become more challenging. Your child may also wish to reverse roles and have you guess the object.

Feeling for recognition. Show your child a variety of familiar objects such as a toy, a comb, or a small book. You can let her feel the objects. Put the objects in a bag or sock where your child can't see them. Have her reach into the bag and touch the object, but don't let her see it. Ask her to determine what the object is. In another version of this game, you can place several objects in the bag or sock, and ask you child to find a specific object or to identify each object.

Playing with blocks. To develop visual thinking skills, use a set of blocks of various sizes, colors, and geometric shapes in the following ways:

- Hold up a block, and ask the child to select another that matches the shape or color of your block.

- Construct a design, using only two or three blocks at first. Have your child duplicate the design.

- Make two identical designs with blocks. Then hide the designs from your child and remove a block from one of the designs. Have your child determine which block is missing and replace it in the design.

- Let your child look at a very simple block design for a few minutes. Then cover the design and ask your child to reconstruct it.

- Lay blocks in a line to form a pattern, such as red, blue, blue, red. Ask your child to select a block to continue the pattern.

Grouping objects. Cut out triangles, circles, and squares in three different colors. Ask your child to sort them into groups. You may give the child three boxes to indicate that there should be three groupings. Most children will group the objects by color. Help your child discover that the objects can also be grouped by shape.

Developing memory skills. Use a deck of Old Maid cards or make a deck that has pairs of different colors or numbers. Adjust the size of the playing deck to your child's memory skills to play this memory game:

1. Place the shuffled cards face down in rows.

2. Turn over two cards to find a matching pair.

3. Put nonmatching cards face down again.

4. Remove matching cards from the game.

5. Continue the game until all cards are matched.

This game can be played alone or with several players.

Identifying colors. Get squares of color samples from a paint shop or make your own squares in a variety of colors to play this game. Mix up the squares. Each player is given a square and must find an object that closely matches its color. Be sure to choose the squares so success is guaranteed.

Sequencing events. Give your child practice in putting events in order through activities such as these:

- Read a story to the child and ask what happened after an event in the story. For example, ask what happened after Goldilocks sat in Baby Bear's chair.

- Ask your child to tell what needs to be done before routine events such as eating lunch or going to bed.

27

Above All Else

Has your child smelled a rose or petted a toad? Has your child played, talked, or worked with people outside the family? Children learn about the world through experience and social interaction. In this way, they build their minds and learn thinking skills. Don't rob them of those opportunities by having them do workbooks and worksheets.

Chapter Four

BUSY FINGERS

Color the car red. Copy the square. Cut out the house. These familiar kindergarten tasks require the use of small muscles and are known as fine motor skills. Such manipulatory skills require control, coordination, and dexterity, especially in the muscles of the hands and fingers.

From the moment children enter the kindergarten classroom, they will use their fine motor skills to color, cut, paste, paint, and, more important, write. Children who lag in developing fine motor skills will face considerable difficulty in printing their names and will have trouble writing during their first years in school. These children will also find it difficult to perform everyday activities such as tying shoes and fastening buttons.

What Children Need to Learn

Fine motor skills are harder to learn and require more practice to develop than other motor skills. It takes people over twenty years to perfect their fine motor skills; however, the first six or seven years are the most critical in developing the basic skills. Your child may not be judged in school by how he colors, copies, pastes, or cuts, but his ability to do these tasks will make a major difference in learning how to write legibly, which is important to teachers.

Teachers realize that children entering school are still developing their fine motor skills and do not expect them to paint like Rembrandt or write their names like John Hancock. But remember: teachers rated fine motor skills as the third most important skill that children should have before entering school (see page 3). Use the checklist on pages 30–31 to see which fine motor skills your child already possesses and to determine the areas where additional practice would be helpful.

Checklist of expected fine motor skills

	can easily accomplish	can accomplish with difficulty	cannot accomplish
Birth to 15 months			
Uses reaching and holding reflexes			
Puts objects in hands and mouth			
Picks up objects with a palm grasp			
Grasps and releases an object			
Handles objects with either hand			
Transfers object from one hand to the other			
Likes manipulating small objects			
Uses spoon as tool to bring food to his mouth			
Uses one finger to poke or push an object			
Tears paper			
Stacks blocks			
Uses thumb and forefinger			
Crams many objects into hands			
Turns pages in a book			
By 2½ years			
Uses a palm grasp when scribbling			
Uses thumb and forefinger to grasp an object			
Drinks out of a sipper cup			
Throws a large ball			
Shows a hand preference			
Uses a marker on paper			
Uses a pegboard			
Strings beads			
Squeezes a toy			
Turns knobs			
Works velcro			
Handles snaps			
Screws on tops			

By 5 years	can easily accomplish	can accomplish with difficulty	cannot accomplish
Manipulates small objects with both hands			
Builds with building toys			
Kneads dough			
Cuts with scissors			
Holds crayons appropriately			
Colors a picture			
Draws a person with at least six body parts			
Traces, copies, and draws basic shapes			
Folds triangles from squares			
Copies a design			
Copies a letter			
Pastes objects on a piece of paper			
Cuts out simple shapes			
Writes numerals 1 to 5			
Uses a fork correctly			
Laces shoes			
Ties knots			
Buttons a coat			
Paints a picture			
Pounds in pegs with control			
Picks up and fits objects together with ease			
Pours liquid into a glass without spilling			
Puts a ten-piece puzzle together			
Makes shadow shapes on the wall			
Spreads peanut butter on a piece of bread			

How Children Learn Fine Motor Skills

Children have their own time clocks that dictate the development of their fine motor skills. How adept they become at using these skills, however, depends on how much they practice using them. Reaching and grasping are fine motor skills that newborns quickly and automatically acquire. Even two-week-old babies reaching for an object make contact 40 percent of the time. Over the weeks and months, fine motor skills develop as children use their arms, hands, and fingers to reach, grasp, and retrieve desired objects. By one year, children can pick up objects with their thumbs and forefingers and are manipulating the objects to study them more closely. Between three and six years, small muscle coordination develops rapidly until the child has acquired the basic fine motor skills that allow him to color, copy, and cut.

Creating a Learning Environment

Infants don't need to be taught to reach or grasp, nor do older children usually need to be taught fine motor skills. Children use their small muscles to grasp things that they want to explore. Your role as a parent is to provide a stimulating environment that will encourage your child to continue using the fine motor skills he has acquired. With practice, your child's skills will improve, and he will be ready to handle the activities of kindergarten that involve manipulating objects.

You should have objects such as the following around the house that are fun for children to use and that encourage the use of small muscles in their hands and fingers:

Art Materials

beads to string	finger paint
chalkboards	music boxes
clay or playdough	paper to tear
coloring books	scissors
crayons	tracing paper

Kitchen Materials

cookie cutters	napkins
dry macaroni, beans	peanut butter to spread
egg beaters	pots and pans
finger food	spoons
measuring spoons	tongs

Household and Clothing Materials

books and magazines	knobs to turn
coats to button	old shoes to lace
coats to zip	pipe cleaners
coins	playing cards
cotton balls	typewriters

Games and Toys

building bricks (Legos)	pictures to lace
dolls to dress	puzzles
miniature cars and dolls	sand tray
nesting blocks	shape sorting box
pegboards	shape stacker

Activities for You and Your Child

Parents should encourage fine motor development through a wealth of activities to help advance their children from infants grasping rattles to preschoolers ready to learn how to button coats, tie shoes, color pictures, and print their names. The following activities will help your child develop the precision, balance, and hand-eye coordination that are needed to perform the fine motor skills required in kindergarten.

From birth to 15 months

Grasping objects. Encourage grasping by placing interesting, brightly colored objects within reach of your child and with activities such as the following:

- Place one of your fingers or a rattle in the palm of the baby's hand. Your baby will use small muscles when tightening his fingers around the object.

- Shake a favorite rattle in front of your child. Hold the toy close enough so that the baby reaches to get it.

Manipulating objects. Hand your baby a toy that makes a noise when squeezed. Give the toy a squeeze so it squeaks. Then wait for the baby to accidentally squeeze the toy. Repeat this activity often, and soon he will squeeze the toy in order to hear the squeak.

Touching objects. Make sure that your baby's arms and hands are free to touch and explore things. Also, have safe objects of different sizes, such as spoons, rubber balls, and rattles available so that he will be able to practice grasping as well as touching.

Making discoveries. Give your baby a shiny pan. At first, he will enjoy looking at himself. Then give him a spoon and let him discover banging.

Playing Peek-a-Boo. Cover your face with your hands. Let your little fingers extend out from your hands. When your baby touches your little fingers, open your hands and say, "peek-a-boo." Soon your baby will start grasping your little fingers and pulling your hands away.

From 15 months to 2½ years

Playing finger rhymes. Teach your child finger rhymes. You can create your own or try some of these childhood favorites:

I'm a Little Teapot

I'm a little teapot,
Short and stout.
Here is my handle. (Put hand on hip).
Here is my spout. (Curve other arm like a spout.)
When I get all steamed up, hear me shout.
Tip me over and pour me out. (Bend sideways.)

Church and Steeple

Here is the church. (Intertwine fingers so that they're hidden.)
Here is the steeple. (Raise and touch pointer fingers.)
Open the door and here's all the people. (Open hands and wiggle fingers.)

Pat-a-Cake

Pat-a-cake, pat-a-cake, baker's man. (Clap own hands.)
Bake me a cake as fast as you can. (Pat child's hands.)
Roll it. (Roll hands.)
And pat it. (Pat back of own hand.)
Mark it with a B. (Draw a B in the air.)
Put it in the oven (Open imaginary oven door.)
for baby and me. (Point to child and self.)

Maneuvering pegs. Make or buy a pegboard and lots of fat pegs to go in it. Show your child how to take the pegs out of the board. When all of the pegs have been removed, let the child discover things to do with the pegs, such as putting them in bottles. It may take weeks before your child is interested in putting the pegs back in the holes. As he gets past the age of putting objects in his mouth, you may want to buy smaller pegs.

Stringing beads. You need a sturdy shoestring and large beads. Tie a large knot in one end of the shoestring and make sure that the other end has a plastic tip or a piece of tape on it so that it can pass easily through the bead. Show your child how to put a bead on the shoestring and guide the child until he is able to string beads. Expand this activity by stringing a pattern of beads and encouraging your child to copy it. Let older children string cereal or hollow noodles on a shoestring.

Feeling objects. Find pairs of familiar objects and put one member of each pair in a bag or covered box. Have your child feel one visible object and then try to find its hidden mate by feeling the objects in the bag or box. Continue until the child has matched all of the pairs. At first, you may only want to use two or three pairs of objects.

Using a sand tray. Draw a simple pattern in the sand and ask your child to copy it. When your child is four or five years old, you can trace patterns of shapes, numerals, or letters in the sand to copy. The child also will enjoy making different kinds of patterns in the sand.

Using a chalkboard. Just having a chalkboard encourages a child to scribble—a vital step in learning handwriting. Show your child how to hold chalk like a writing instrument with the thumb and index finger on top of the piece of chalk and the middle finger on the bottom. Your child will probably not elect to hold it this way at first. Do not be concerned, but continue to demonstrate the appropriate way to hold the chalk from time to time. Like a sand tray, the chalkboard can be used to trace objects, letters, and numerals, as well as to draw pictures. When your child reaches elementary school age, the chalkboard can be used to write the weekly spelling words and to practice math facts.

Lacing cards. Make lacing cards by cutting pictures from magazines or coloring books and gluing them onto pieces of cardboard. Cover the cardboard with clear contact paper and punch several holes around the outline of the pictures. Tie a knot in a shoestring or heavy yarn behind one of the holes. Make sure that the other end of the string can easily be pulled through the holes (you can glue the end of the yarn to make it hard).

From 2½ to 5 years

Drawing. Start your child drawing before his first birthday and, by two and a half, his drawings of people should begin to look like crude stick people. When your child is three, you can give him circles and the letter X to copy.

Using crayons and felt markers. As soon as your child stops putting everything in his mouth, give him crayons. Have your child use the jumbo crayons at first. By two and a half, children also enjoy using felt markers. Provide your child with lots of paper and let his creativity control what is drawn. Do not expect works of art—your child is more interested in the process than in creating a masterpiece.

Finger painting. Your child can finger paint in anything from pudding to catsup. Just drop a blob of the special "paint" on a large piece of paper and encourage him to use his fingers to make dots, lines, circles, or whatever designs tickle his fancy. To make finger paint, combine one-fourth cup of liquid laundry starch with a few drops of food coloring.

Painting. Spend some time helping your child learn how to hold a brush and how to avoid dripping paint. It is a good idea to have your child begin by using poster paints. Instead of buying a variety of colors, encourage him to combine colors to form others.

Opening and closing objects. Make an activity board for your child by covering a board with contact paper and placing objects on it that open and close. Use hooks and eyes, velcro fasteners, and several kinds of locks. Make sure that the lock keys are on a sturdy piece of string fastened to the board so that they will not be misplaced.

Sewing. After your child learns to lace pictures, teach him a simple running stitch. Then have him make a bean bag, using a running stitch around four sides of two pieces of material. Next have him draw several X's on a piece of paper and teach him to follow the marks with a simple cross-stitch.

Playing games. Play Pick-up Sticks with your child. In this game, each of you picks up one stick at a time without disturbing others in the pile. Next, each of you can try dropping beads into a wide-mouthed container from different heights.

Using a pencil. When your child is ready, buy a pencil holder that slides on pencils so that he is required to hold the pencil correctly.

Above All Else

You can play a major role in your child's successful growth from tight-fisted infant to scribbling preschooler. The secret lies in presenting your child with an environment that encourages the use of hands and fingers in all kinds of activities from finger painting to picking up crumbs from the kitchen floor.

Chapter Five

PLAYING FAIR AND SHARING

No biting. No kicking. No grabbing another child's toys. Don't interrupt someone who is talking. Don't say hurtful things. Children won't follow these commonsense social rules automatically. They must learn them, and it's usually up to parents to teach them to their preschool children.

Social skills are an absolute must for success in school. They are a bridge for all the other learning that takes place. Imagine a first grader in a reading group: there will be problems if the child talks all the time, hogs the teacher's attention, or knocks classmates' books on the floor. It is the same at all levels in school. How successful will a high school group project be if several students are too shy to make any contributions?

What Children Need to Learn

Kindergarten teachers don't expect children to behave like miniature adults, but they do expect them to have certain key social skills to build on in kindergarten. Your child needs to grow from a self-centered infant to a preschooler conscious of the needs of others. She needs to be able to interact effectively with the teacher and the other children.

Children do not do well in school just because they are smart. They also need to get along with others. Use the checklist on pages 40–41 to see if your child is acquiring the social skills needed for kindergarten.

How Children Learn Social Skills

Parents are primarily responsible for teaching their children social skills. Do an inadequate job, and your child's behavior may be unacceptable to her teachers or peers. (Of course, all children will behave unacceptably at times, even with proper training from parents.) A child with very poor social skills could be labeled a social misfit in kindergarten. In that case, considerable classroom time must be devoted to teaching the child appropriate school behavior before work on the regular curriculum can begin.

Children aren't born with social skills but acquire them through interaction first with their families and then with the world outside the home. Like thinking skills, your child's social skills will develop in stages.

Infants socialize from birth

Infants are helpless beings completely dependent on their parents or caregivers for survival. They do, however, play an active role in their own social development. Infants communicate what they want by crying or cooing. At the same time, they read reactions—the smiles, hugs, cuddles, and comfort given them. The smoother the interaction between parent and child, the more sociable an infant becomes.

By six to eight months of age, the child is primarily attached to one person. This relationship gives the child a safe base from which to explore the world. By ten months, the child will look to this person for clues about how to handle new situations: a stranger, a barking dog, or a new toy. During this first stage of social development, from birth to eighteen months, your child needs to establish a basic sense of safety or trust in her environment through interaction with parents and other caregivers.

Toddlers imitate others

As children leave infancy, they become increasingly, but unevenly, social. Sometimes they act like patient adults, and other times they are frustrated and impatient young children. Their socialization is modeled more than ever on the behavior of others; imitation is in full swing. Toddlers pick up personality traits such as shyness and friendliness from their parents.

Parents can expect children at this age to spend more time playing alongside rather than with other children. They can also expect to see the beginnings of rudimentary sharing. If given a toy, toddlers will give their playmate another toy. They will also try to influence the behavior of other children by smiles and vocalizations.

Checklist of expected social skills

	can easily accomplish	can accomplish with difficulty	cannot accomplish
Birth to 15 months			
Waves bye-bye			
Imitates behavior of parents and caretakers			
Responds to or imitates games such as Pat-a-Cake			
Anticipates feeding, dressing, and bathing			
Distinguishes between familiar people and strangers			
Adapts to changing people and places			
Shows considerable interest in peers			
Enjoys exploring objects with another person			
Gets others to do things for her pleasure			
Gives and takes objects			
By 2½ years			
Imitates behavior of peers and adults			
Plays alongside another child			
Calls some children friends			
Enjoys small group activities for short periods of time			
Starts to see benefits of cooperation			
Has some awareness of the feelings of others			
Shows some control of impulses in dealing with others			
Starts to recognize that others have rights and privileges			
Begins to assert self appropriately in some situations			

	can easily accomplish	can accomplish with difficulty	cannot accomplish
By 5 years			
Approaches new people with interest			
Begins to show awareness of similarities and differences among people			
Begins to have empathy for others			
Begins to function as a group member			
Uses play to explore social roles			
Manages peer conflict constructively			
Begins to share with others			
Starts to take turns			
Functions as a leader or follower in play situations			
Does not interfere with the work of others			
Asserts rights appropriately			
Begins to follow rules			
Recognizes authority			
Makes appropriate social responses			
Seeks help when needed			

Preschoolers make friends

From ages three to five, children become increasingly competent at socializing with others, even though the family remains the hub of their universe. They are now ready to form ties with other children. While three-year-olds still like to remain near familiar adults when they are playing, four- and five-year-olds look to their playmates for approval. They begin to have friends and to use these new relationships as a safe base for exploring unfamiliar territory.

Creating a Learning Environment

The first step in building your child's social skills is to create a loving bond with the child from infancy. This occurs most easily when you are emotionally expressive toward her, with lots of smiles, hugs, loving touches, and verbal communication. You should also be sensitive to your baby's signals. Respond to her laughs, smiles, and distress signals. There can never be too much close contact between infant and parent.

Your child will first show interest in other children at around six months of age. At this age, she will just look at or perhaps imitate other children. By one year, your child will begin to show interest in playing with others. That is the time to make sure that she has contact with other children the same age. By two, your child should be ready for a small play group. Lots of toys are needed for these groups because the children aren't really ready to share, and supervision will be needed to avoid unpleasant experiences. Your child will often prefer to play with one friend in a familiar place.

Your three-year-old will want playmates. You won't have to encourage them to play. Just make sure that they have plenty of simple toys and a safe play area. Stay in the background unless things start to get out of control. Let the children work out how to get along together. Your child's social skills will improve the most when she plays with the same children every day. By four, most children can play reasonably well with friends, so if she is not already in one, you may wish to have your child attend a nursery school to ensure daily contact with other children. This will help her become more socially adept.

Activities for You and Your Child

Your child will begin to learn social skills within the family setting. She will then build upon those skills outside the family by playing with other children. Choose the appropriate play activities to enhance your child's social skills.

From birth to 15 months

Playing Copycat. Respond to your infant's burblings, cooings, and other sounds. Initiate communication by repeating the first sounds your child makes. Infants are attracted to the sound of the human voice. The more you talk to your child the easier it will be to establish a bond.

Waving bye-bye. When someone is leaving your home, get in the habit of saying, "bye-bye." At the same time, help your child wave bye-bye. By nine to twelve months, after many repetitions of bye-bye and a wave, your child will have learned a social gesture and start waving bye-bye on her own.

Meeting another baby. When children first meet, always introduce them to each other. Even if your child is only six months old, tell her the other child's name. Put the children near each other and give them similar toys. Don't expect them to play together, but you can expect them to imitate each other's play. You should supervise the children and be ready to solve any disputes by handing the unhappy child a similar toy.

From 15 months to 2½ years

Learning to cooperate. Encourage your child to become interested in helping you dress her by asking her to get shoes, socks, sweaters, and other articles of clothing that are to be worn. Let your child do as much dressing or undressing as she can handle. At this age children are usually better at undressing than dressing.

Playing simple games. One way for your child to learn small group activities is through games such as Ring Around the Rosy or Musical Chairs. There must not be any element of winning or losing in these games, and the more movement, the better. Be sure to join the children in playing games: they will love to see you fall down or struggle to find a chair.

Ring Around the Rosy

Ring around the rosy,   (Children join hands and skip in a circle.)
A pocket full of posies,
Ashes, ashes, we all fall down.   (Children drop hands and fall to floor.)

Musical Chairs

Set the same number of chairs as there are children back to back in a line. Players circle the chairs as music is played. When the music stops, each child rushes to choose a chair. Be sure there is always a chair for each child.

Developing concern for others' feelings. Point out other peoples' feelings to your child. Say, for example, "Sarah is unhappy because you took away her favorite toy." "George is sad because he lost his balloon." "Grandmother is happy because we came to visit her." Your statements will help your children recognize other people's feelings.

Behaving properly in social situations. Children gain confidence when they know how to behave in social situations. When they start to talk, it is easy for them to learn when to say "please," "thank you," and "excuse me." They also can learn good behavior if you playact with them how to greet people and how to act in new situations, such as visiting a sit-down restaurant.

From 2½ to 5 years

Learning to function as a leader and a follower. Encourage your child to play games such as Farmer in the Dell; Mother, May I; and Follow the Leader. Playing Follow the Leader gives a child a chance to learn both what being a leader feels like and how to follow the directions of others.

Farmer in the Dell

A group of children forms a circle around one child who plays the "farmer" and begins singing the song on the following page. The farmer chooses another child to be the "wife," the wife chooses someone to be the "child," and so on. The last child chosen plays the "cheese" and becomes the next farmer.

The farmer in the dell,
The farmer in the dell,
Heigh-ho, the derry-o,
The farmer in the dell.

The farmer takes a wife (or husband)...
The wife takes a child...
The child takes a nurse...
The nurse takes the dog...
The dog takes the cat...
The cat takes the rat...
The rat takes the cheese...
The cheese stands alone...

Mother May I?

The child who plays "Mother" stands about fifteen feet away from the other children. Mother calls each person's name in turn, saying, "You may take one giant step" (or any number of baby steps, hops, or scissor steps). Before stepping forward, the named child must ask, "Mother, may I?" Mother replies, "Yes, you may." If the child forgets to ask, she must return to the starting line. The first child to get close enough to tag Mother becomes the next Mother. Players may sneak steps, but if Mother notices, she can send them back.

Follow the Leader

Children and adults can take turns being the leader. Everyone else follows and copies the leader as she walks, marches, hops, tiptoes, claps, touches her nose, etc.

Dressing up or playacting. Your child needs to try many social roles. Kitchen utensils, toy tools, and dress-up clothes and accessories (from a cook's apron to a doctor's stethoscope) should be available so that the child has props to act out familiar events or scenes. Make sure she has dolls with which to act out child-care scenes.

Learning "good manners." Having good manners means having consideration for others. This is the social skill your child needs most. Children easily acquire good manners by imitating their parents' behavior. Model good manners by including your child in conversations you have with other adults or asking her preferences regarding dress, food, and play instead of always imposing your choices.

Above All Else

Be warm and loving with your child if you want her to get along well with others. And have certain rules of social behavior that you expect her to follow. Without rules or control, your child is likely to become aggressive toward other children and may rebel against the teacher's rules. Don't be afraid to state rules. They will be most effective if a reason is given that stresses the feelings of others. Say, "You must not hit people." Then be sure to add, "If you hit Matthew, it will hurt him."

Chapter Six

ZIP, BUTTON, AND TIE

It's a rainy day, and there are twenty children in your child's kindergarten class. At recess time, the teacher faces the task of bundling them all into coats, hats, boots, and anything else parents expect them to wear. Fifteen minutes later, the outdoor clothes must all come off again. Is it any wonder the teacher hopes not to hear, "But teacher, I need help!"

What Children Need to Learn

Teachers may not expect children to read or write on the first day of school, but they certainly expect them to have the self-help skills needed to go to the bathroom without assistance; wash their hands; and put on their coats, hats, and mittens. Self-help skills such as these enable children to survive at school when their parents are not around to wipe their noses, remind them to go to the bathroom, or pour their milk. Fortunately, teachers do not expect children to have every self-help skill mastered, and they are willing to help small hands with buttons and zippers.

Use the checklist on page 48 to see which self-help skills your child has learned and which ones still need to be learned before he starts school.

How Children Learn Self-Help Skills

From infancy onward, your child is on a quest for autonomy. Given the freedom to try to do things for themselves, children will be on the right path. Children whose parents are always eager to tie their shoes or button their pants will be slower to acquire self-help skills.

Checklist of expected self-help skills

	can easily accomplish	can accomplish with difficulty	cannot accomplish
Birth to 15 months			
Has developed senses			
Looks at a body part when it is touched			
Places objects in hands			
Clasps hands and fingers together			
Begins to use a spoon			
By 2½ years			
Attempts to go to the bathroom without help			
Washes hands			
Combs hair			
Brushes teeth			
Puts on socks			
Puts on shoes			
Feeds self			
By 5 years			
Completes toilet skills			
Dresses and undresses self completely			
Washes face and hands			
Knows how to use a handkerchief or tissue			
Fastens buckles			
Buttons shirts, pants, and coats			
Zips zippers			
Opens and closes snaps			
Puts on boots			
Puts on gloves or mittens			
Uses a spoon or fork effectively			
Uses a knife for spreading			
Pours a drink			
Takes toys out to play with them			
Puts toys away			

Parents should expect children to progress gradually in their desire to do boring, repetitive self-help chores. For example, children who wash their faces at three with their parents' guidance will do it alone, when asked, at four. At five, you hope they will wash their faces because they are dirty.

With each year, children become more eager to take care of themselves. Toddlers resent being treated like babies. They don't want people to push and pull their clothes on them when they can do most of the job without help. They definitely want to feed themselves. Given the opportunity to take care of their own needs, most children are eager to acquire the necessary skills as soon as they are developmentally ready.

Creating a Learning Environment

A baby's first steps are thrilling for any parent to watch. But it is not always easy to accept the independence that your child acquires along with self-help skills. Even so, you must give him the opportunity to become independent.

You need to have the patience and willingness to let your child try and try again until each self-help skill is mastered. Encouragement is especially important when you hear your child say, "I want to do it." "Yes, I can." "Let me do it." "Don't hold me." "I'm not a baby." At first it will be hard not to jump in and get a task done. You may also find it difficult not to redo tasks, such as combing hair or washing hands, that have not been done to your standards.

Nevertheless, this is the way your child will learn to take care of himself. You can make it easier for your child to master self-help skills by giving him possible tasks to accomplish. Most two-year-olds simply don't have the fine motor skills to tie their shoes. And most three-year-olds will not use handkerchiefs. When your child is learning a new skill, you can help by breaking a task down into simple steps so that the task is more manageable. You can also help by allowing sufficient time for completing a task, since rushing will only upset and frustrate your child.

You will want to have toys in your home that help your preschooler practice the skills needed for dressing. Dolls with buttons, zippers, and snaps can be bought for this purpose, or an old shirt and pants can be mounted on a board for buttoning and zipping practice. Be sure that the buttons and zippers are large enough for your child to manipulate easily.

You also need to arrange your home so that it is easy for your child to acquire self-help skills. Halls and bathrooms need nightlights so that your child is more willing to go to the bathroom at night. Make sure that bathroom doors are easy to open and that your child can reach his toothbrush, toothpaste, comb, and brush. Dresser drawers should be easy to open. Store toys so that your child can easily get them out and put them back.

Activities for You and Your Child

Self-help skills are needed in activities that range from toilet training to fixing a snack. The more you encourage and support your child's efforts to acquire these skills, the sooner he will acquire them. But be careful not to push him into attempting tasks that he is not ready for, which could make him disinterested or afraid to try these tasks later on. Follow your child's interests in selecting activities that will put him on the road to independence.

From birth to 15 months

Holding a cup. This activity will help your child get accustomed to using a drinking cup. While he is watching, show your child how to hold and drink out of a cup. Remember to tell him what you are doing as you do it. (Then give the cup to him every day after he has eaten, encouraging him to lift the cup.) When he starts to bring the cup to his mouth, add a little juice or water, and he will learn that something is in the cup. Don't limit this activity to mealtimes; try it at snack times, too.

Helping to get dressed. Even a baby can help with getting dressed. Encourage your child to move his arms and legs to help you as you dress him. Explain what is going to happen next and how he can help you. Say, for example, "I'm going to put your socks on now. Lift up a foot for me."

Eating with a spoon. This activity is a messy one, so place a plastic drop cloth under the high chair. When your child begins grabbing at the spoon during feeding time, give him a spoon to hold and attempt to use. Although most children begin trying to spoon-feed themselves at one, they won't be truly proficient at spoon-feeding until two.

From 15 months to 2½ years

Washing. Most toddlers and preschoolers enjoy baths so much that parents have trouble getting them out of the tub. But bath time can be more than just water fun: you can teach children how to lather. Just as important as learning how to wash is learning how to rinse off soap. Make a game out of washing by having the child wash different body parts as you name them.

A *cautionary note:* Never leave your child alone in the bathtub even for an instant.

Brushing teeth. If your child watches you brush your teeth and begs to try it, you have an excellent opportunity to introduce the correct way to brush. Provide your child with a child-sized toothbrush and let him start brushing (without toothpaste at first).

Combing and brushing hair. Once your child expresses interest in combing or brushing his hair, provide combs and brushes that are small enough for easy handling. Then suggest that he style a doll's hair for additional practice in these skills.

From 2½ to 5 years

Asking for help. Your child needs to know phrases to use when he wants help. If you say, "Will you help me?" and "Please help me" when you request help, he will become accustomed to hearing these phrases and start using them himself. And when your child does say, "I'd like some help," be sure to ask, "How can I help?" instead of automatically completing the task. Then the child will not only know help is available and feel more confident asking for it, but will also become more adept at telling you what kind of help he needs.

Dressing up. Provide your child with a play wardrobe of adult clothing. When he plays dress-up, he is getting additional practice in learning how to dress.

Toilet training. Children need to be mentally and physically ready before they begin toilet training. Most children will master this skill by three, with girls usually being trained before boys. Remember, toilet training requires considerable time and patience on the parents' part. Your child should have mastered some other self-help skills such as brushing teeth or washing hands before he begins toilet training. He also needs to have seen other people using the toilet and shown some signs of imitating their behavior. Be sure that your child is wearing pants that can be pulled down easily.

Talk about the process of going to the bathroom with your child. If he is ready for toilet training, he probably wants to be independent, so make sure that he is in charge of the process. Try to be be consistent about the time the child goes. Right after meals or whenever he usually needs diapers changed are good times because your chances for success are better. Don't expect the child to master toilet training immediately, but when he is successful, applaud him vigorously.

Buttoning and zipping. One of the first steps to independent dressing is working fasteners. Children need to be shown each step. Begin by having your child watch you push a large button halfway through a large buttonhole. (This is a good skill for children to practice in the car.) Then show him how to pull the button through the hole. The two of you can take turns pushing and pulling the button through the hole until your child wants to try buttoning his own clothes.

Children can start learning to work a zipper by pulling up a zipper as you hold the bottom of a jacket or sweater together. Next, show your child how to hold the bottom of the jacket together before trying to zip it up. Your child can practice buttoning and zipping skills on dolls or by using self-help toys designed to teach these skills.

Acquiring table manners. Children learn through example. If they hear their parents use the words "please" and "thank you" at the dinner table, they will start using these words too. In the same way, children will imitate their parents' use of silverware. For additional practice, encourage your child to playact eating situations.

Caring for fingernails. Children cannot cut their own nails, but they enjoy learning how to file their nails with an emery board, and they especially like using a nail brush to scrub their nails.

Above All Else

Don't handicap your child by doing too much for him. As soon as your child shows an interest in helping himself, teach him how. Then be very patient while he practices and practices before finally acquiring each skill.

Chapter Seven

HAPPY AWAY FROM HOME

Good-bye, Mommy. Good-bye, Daddy. Good-bye, familiar home and favorite playthings. Hello, strange new building. Hello, new adults telling me what to do. Hello, new group of peers.

It's time for your child to start school. It is not easy for a young child to adjust to the many changes that involves and settle down happily in the classroom. Will your child be happy away from home? Yes, if she feels good about herself. Experts call this having a good self-image, positive self-concept, or high self-esteem. Feeling good about herself makes a child confident that she can meet the demands of school.

Nothing is linked more closely to poor school performance than a lack of self-esteem. Children with negative self-images often feel they have nothing to offer teachers and classmates and expect others to take advantage of them. They usually get lower grades and have fewer friends than those with high self-esteem.

What Children Need to Learn

Children need to learn that the people closest to them think highly of them. In fact, at all ages one's self-esteem is closely tied to the judgments of others. Even young children know whether they are thought of as stupid or clever, helpless or capable, annoying or delightful, clumsy or agile.

Self-esteem is closely tied to whether your child will face the challenges of school with confidence or trepidation. Use the checklist on pages 56–57 to evaluate the progress your child is making in acquiring a good self-image.

How Children Develop Self-Esteem

Children aren't born with self-esteem. It develops over time. Children go through stages in which they learn more about themselves and gradually establish their unique identities.

Stage one: infancy

Infants don't truly recognize themselves as separate individuals: mother and infant are one. But as infants interact with others, they figure out that they exist independently of others. Researchers test self-image in infants by placing them in front of a mirror. Between five and eight months, children enjoy looking in the mirror and will often try to touch their reflection. By twelve months, children will wave at the mirror, making their image do what they are doing. This doesn't mean that the children actually recognize themselves in the mirror. For most children, this does not happen until they are eighteen months old and are able to distinguish between pictures of themselves and pictures of others.

Stage two: toddlers and preschoolers

During this stage, two- and three-year-olds struggle to become independent, while newly independent four- and five-year-olds eagerly acquire new skills, such as buttoning and doing puzzles, and take pride in their accomplishments. Now is the time children establish their identities as separate and distinct individuals. They begin to notice how people differ, and they place themselves and others in broad categories by age, size, and gender. Anyone under age six is a little boy or girl while anyone over fifty is a grandmother or grandfather. If asked to describe themselves, preschoolers often respond with a description of something they do, such as set the table or swim.

Helping your child develop self-esteem

Your infant or toddler's feeling of self-esteem is closely tied to how you judge her. Is she a joy or a nuisance, precious or pesky? Preschoolers, however, need more than approval of their existence to continue developing self-esteem. They also need to feel that they are successful in mastering their environment and in mastering their emotions. In addition, they need to feel that you believe they are successful.

A cautionary note: Children measure personal success in terms of mastering skills that are important to them, such as stacking blocks, riding a tricycle, or putting on a sweater. Don't compromise their feelings of success by valuing only their mastery of skills that are important to you, such as counting, reciting poems, or coloring perfectly

Checklist of expected self-esteem skills

	can easily accomplish	can accomplish with difficulty	cannot accomplish
Birth to 15 months			
Shows intense feelings for parents			
Shows affection for familiar person through hugs and smiles			
Shows pride and pleasure in mastering tasks			
Expresses clearly differentiated emotions such as pleasure, disappointment, anger, fear, joy, and excitement			
Puts self to sleep			
Begins to quiet self			
Asserts self			
By 2½ years			
Differentiates facial expressions of anger, sadness, and joy			
Demonstrates awareness of own feelings			
Demonstrates awareness of others' feelings			
Expresses feelings through dramatic play			
Verbalizes feelings			
Shows increased control of emotions			
Begins to sense what is acceptable and unacceptable behavior			
Shows pride in new accomplishments			
Begins to appreciate own competency			
Has emerging sense of self			

	can easily accomplish	can accomplish with difficulty	cannot accomplish
By 5 years			
Begins to recognize and label emotions such as anger, happiness, sadness, and fear			
Expresses both positive and negative feelings			
Has knowledge of own gender and ethnic background			
Has initiative to try new things			
Acts confident in new situations			
Makes decisions			
Postpones gratification			
Begins to exercise self-control			
Is not easily frustrated			
Does not cry easily			
Displays even temper			
Understands the idea of acceptable behavior			
Does not require constant support from parents or caregivers			
Separates from parents without being upset			
Starts to understand own strengths and limitations			
Has strong and positive sense of self			

within lines. Try to support their efforts to master the skills important to them.

Discipline and self-esteem

Children want to do what is right. Good discipline will not only help your child learn self-control but will also build her self-esteem. Good discipline will encourage her to cooperate, allow her gradually to take responsibility for her behavior, and help her to solve problems. Bad approaches to discipline will tear down her self-esteem. By making your child do something because you're bigger and stronger, you crush her fledgling sense of confidence. By making the child feel that it is she, rather than what she's done, that is unsatisfactory, you create self-doubt. Constant arguments and a daily diet of "no's" do the same thing. Save your discipline for issues that really matter.

All children rebel against authority. They want to be in charge of their behavior. The best discipline will allow your child some control over her life. The preschool years are the time for you to give your child more control and to teach her how to make choices. Let her decide between two acceptable choices, rather than simply forbidding the unacceptable choice. For example, when in situations where you can't allow your preschooler to roam around by herself, give her the option of holding your hand or riding in a stroller, rather than just placing her in the stroller.

Independence and self-esteem

The transition from dependent infant to independent child occurs as the child masters language and physical skills, learns to play with other children, and begins to show self-control. The more you teach your child about how to take care of herself, the greater confidence your child will have to move out into the world.

A cautionary note: Parents who fear having their child go to school may prevent the child from developing independence by trying to hold on to their "baby." They may keep dressing and bathing a child long after she is capable of accomplishing these tasks by herself. They may also step in too soon when the child is having problems with other children. When parents do too much for a preschooler, the child loses confidence in her ability to handle the world and her self-esteem plummets.

Creating a Learning Environment

Don't be silent; be verbal about what your child accomplishes. You build your child's self-esteem through communication. When the child starts exploring the world, childproof your home so she can become independent. As she begins to show interest in taking care of herself, foster that interest by giving her the opportunity to learn self-help skills. If you keep putting on her shoes when she wants to try, she will remain dependent on you. Let your preschooler do as much as she can for herself; step in to help only when necessary.

Activities for You and Your Child

The route that leads to self-esteem and a child who is happy to leave home and go to school is a route you and your child travel together. You must be her reassuring guide. The following activities will help your child be ready for the emotional challenges of school.

From birth to 15 months

Exploring self-awareness. By five months, your child will enjoy looking in a mirror. Although the child won't truly recognize her reflection until eighteen months, the mirror will be a very responsive playmate. When your child smiles, waves, or moves, the mirror image will always respond. When the child looks in the mirror, tell her who she sees. Playing with a mirror helps your child develop the idea of self.

Building self-esteem. Respond to your infant's needs. Let the child see that you regard child care as a joy, not a chore. Make sure the child knows that she can rely on you, and she will develop trust in you. She needs to learn to trust others before she can trust herself. No matter how she behaves, express approval of her as a person.

Building independence. Put toys on low, open shelves so your child can reach them without adult help. Respect your child's choice of play activity rather than choosing activities for her.

Going to sleep. Establish a regular bedtime and follow a routine that includes reading to the child. Knowing what to expect helps children learn to put themselves to sleep.

Having fun. Play with your child. It will be fun for both of you and increase the pleasure your child has in life. Be sure to find activities you both enjoy whether you are birdwatching or skipping rocks.

From 15 months to 2½ years

Being independent. Be patient when your child wants to start dressing and doing hundreds of other things by herself. Let her put groceries into the cart, feed the cat, and make the beds. Your child won't grow up if she remains dependent on you.

Making simple decisions. Clothing and food are two areas in which your child can easily begin to make decisions. Instead of asking her what she wants to wear or eat, choices that are too broad for this age level, give her two good alternatives: "Do you want to wear your new or old tennis shoes?" "Do you want carrots or peas?" Practice makes a child a good decision maker. Expand your child's decision-making to other areas such as choosing things to do.

Learning about people. Take your child to your workplace. Show the child what you do in a way she can understand. Then let her pretend to be you at work by sitting at a desk, typing into a computer, or standing behind a counter. Children are curious to know what their parents do when they are away from home, and this activity will help your child gain a broader understanding of the world.

Learning about feelings. Express your feelings. Say, "I'm mad because the cat knocked over the plant," or "I'm happy because we are going to the park." Be sure to label your child's feelings, too. Say, "You look happy when you play with Mark." Play pretend games that give your child the opportunity to express emotions.

Differentiating feelings. Faces are expressive. Play a guessing game by asking your child to label your feelings from your actions and expressions. For example, look downcast and ask your child if she thinks you are happy or sad. You can also play this game by having the child study your reflection in a mirror.

From 2½ to 5 years

Talking about feelings. Discuss some everyday events with your child, focusing on their emotional aspects. Ask your child to express how she would feel if someone tore up a picture she drew, if a friend gave her some new crayons, or if another child grabbed a favorite toy. Once your child can express feelings, discuss appropriate behavior to handle the feelings.

Postponing gratification. Children don't come with built-in clocks. They understand "now," not "later" or "someday." Play Wait a Minute to help your child learn to delay gratification. In this game, build a tower of blocks with your child, seeing how tall you can make it. Take turns adding blocks, pausing thirty seconds between each turn. Later, the time can be extended to one minute between turns. Use an hourglass or a timer to mark the time.

Acting out good-bye. Separation from home is easier if children have a chance to playact separation. Encourage your child to act out stories that tell about animals or children who leave their homes, such as *The Runaway Bunny* by Margaret Wise Brown or *Where the Wild Things Are* by Maurice Sendak.

Reading about going to school. The first day of school is much less threatening if children have had stories about school read to them. Here are some books you might like to read with your child:

- B. Benzen. *First Day in School.* New York: Doubleday, 1972.

- Stan and Jan Berenstein. *The Berenstein Bears Go to School.* New York: Random House, 1978.

- E. Bram. *I Don't Want to Go to School.* New York: Greenwillow, 1977.

- J. Hamilton-Merritt. *My First Days of School.* New York: Julian Messner, 1982.

- J. Howe. *When You Go to Kindergarten.* New York: Knopf, 1986.

- Cynthia Jabar. *Alice Ann Gets Ready for School.* Boston: Little, Brown, 1989.

- Amy Schwarts. *Annabelle Swift, Kindergartner.* New York: Orchard Books, 1988.

- Muriel Stanek. *Starting School.* Chicago: Albert Whitman, 1981.

- S. E. Tester. *We Laughed a Lot My First Day of School.* Elgin, IL: The Child's World, 1979.

- R. Wells. *Timothy Goes to School.* New York: Dial Press, 1981.

Above All Else

You want your child to be happy away from home. It will be much easier for the child if she has had many happy times away from home with grandparents, friends, and small play groups before the first day of school. Make sure your child learns what kindergarten will be like through storybooks and actual school visits. Finally, build your child's self-esteem so she feels competent to face new situations with a minimum of anxiety. Your child will develop self-esteem from being appreciated for the person she is.

Chapter Eight

SPEAKING OUT

The kindergarten teacher asks your child, "What is your name?" "Where do you find whales?" "How did Cinderella lose her slipper?" "Why do plants need water?" Teachers never run out of questions. And the questions become harder to answer with each grade in school. Where is Burma? What is the greenhouse effect? What is glasnost? Speaking out in school involves far more than just answering questions about what has been learned. It means sharing thoughts, needs, and feelings with teachers and classmates. It is telling everyone in the kindergarten class about the spiderweb outside a bedroom window. It is explaining to a high-school government class the difference between unicameral and bicameral legislatures. It means asking questions to get information: "Why do tomatoes have seeds?" "How are bricks made?" "When is the history test?" Children who are skillful users of oral language have a decided advantage in school. They shine in class discussions from the first day of school, which builds self-esteem. Furthermore, the better the child's speaking skills, the better his social skills will be.

What Children Need to Learn

By the time your child walks into the kindergarten classroom, he should be able to take an active part in conversations with his teachers and classmates. His speech should be easy to understand. And he should have a vocabulary of approximately 2,000 words to express his needs, thoughts, and feelings.

The speed with which children go from cooing infants to chatterboxes is lightning fast. But because some children are by nature quiet or talkative, all children will not start speaking at the same age or speak as much. Use the checklist on pages 64–65 to evaluate your child's progress in acquiring speaking skills.

Checklist of expected speaking skills

	can easily accomplish	can accomplish with difficulty	cannot accomplish
Birth to 15 months			
Coos and gurgles in infancy			
Repeats same sounds frequently			
Cries differently for different needs			
Babbles, using different sounds			
Uses voice to get attention			
Uses voice to establish social contact			
Enjoys imitating sounds			
Enjoys making sounds of familiar animals and objects			
Laughs a lot			
Says a few words, such as "mama" and "dada"			
By 2½ years			
Uses more words than gestures			
Asks questions			
Responds to simple questions			
Repeats requests			
Names pictures			
Forms some plurals			
Uses two- and three-word sentences ("Eat cookie")			
Carries on conversation with self and dolls			
Refers to self by name			
Begins to verbalize some feelings			
Participates in conversations			

	can easily accomplish	can accomplish with difficulty	cannot accomplish
By 5 years			
Produces understandable speech			
Labels familiar objects, people, and actions			
Defines objects by use (you drink from a glass)			
Uses descriptive words *(large, good, cute)*			
Uses the same sentence structure as family members			
Speaks in complete sentences			
Uses sentences of five to six words			
Asks questions for information			
Gives commands			
Varies intensity and tone of voice appropriately			
Sings simple songs			
Tells about recent personal experiences accurately			
Tells familiar stories			
Makes up pretend stories			

How Children Develop Speaking Skills

Speaking, like walking and reaching, is tied to maturation. Children learn to speak step by step, going from initial babble to that magic first word in about a year. Before children become verbal dynamos, they go through four language acquisition stages.

The babbling stage

The first sounds your baby makes are the familiar vowel-like coos of infants. At about four to five months, your baby starts babbling—making nonsense sounds—by combining vowels and consonants. Besides initiating sounds on their own, infants also babble in response to sounds their parents make in conversation. Infants are ready to speak any language and actually produce sounds that occur in all languages. However, children must hear language spoken in order to acquire speech, so American children soon use only the English sounds they hear.

The one-word stage

Whether a child will speak English, French, or Japanese, his first words appear toward the end of his first year. Most of these words will be nouns representing objects important to the child, such as "balls," "shoes," and "juice." Next come the one word requests: "cookie," "mama," "milk." One word conversations with parents also develop:

>Child: Car.
>Parent: You want to go in the car.
>Child: Go.
>Parent: Let's go for a ride in the car.

Vocabulary growth is slow for three or four months after the first word; a child typically adds only about ten words. Then a new word is added every few days. After a child has picked up about fifty words, the rate of learning accelerates so rapidly that a two-year-old will have learned to say several hundred words.

The two-word stage

Children start putting two words together to form sentences between eighteen and twenty-four months. Parents have to do a lot of guesswork to figure out what is meant by combinations such as "Erin cookie" or "David ball." Children go on from the two-word stage to forming sentences of three or more words.

The short, simple sentence stage

First sentences only have nouns and verbs: "Molly hit ball." "Jacob want car." This is called "telegraphic" speech because children use only the bare essentials. You won't find them using *a, as, by,* or *through;* just the meaty words in sentences. At this point, children also begin teaching themselves grammar, learning first that the usual word order is subject-verb-object. As their sentences become longer and more complex, they figure out how plurals and verb tense work. They become fairly good grammarians by five and will learn how to form increasingly complex sentences with several clauses during elementary school.

Watch for Signs of Problems

Most children acquire good speaking skills easily. You should know, however, that 10 percent of all children in school have speech or language impairments that interfere with their progress. Your preschool child needs to be referred to a speech disorders specialist if you notice any of the following:

- The child is not cooing or babbling by six months.

- The child cannot use a few single words by age one.

- The child cannot put two words together by age two.

- The child cannot combine three words by age two and a half ("me want juice").

- The child omits or substitutes many initial and final consonants after age two and a half.

Source: Stacy Litz, speech language pathologist. Communicology, Inc., Indianapolis, Indiana.

Stuttering is common

It is not unusual for children between the ages of two and four to say "I g-g-go" or "I go, I go, I go." They may be thinking faster than they can speak, or they may not yet have complete control of their speech organs. For most children, stuttering only lasts a few months and gradually disappears. When your child repeats sounds or words, follow these steps to prevent it from becoming a real problem:

1. Let your child talk.

2. Don't call attention to the stuttering.

3. Don't interrupt or show impatience when the child is talking.

4. Never say, "Speak more slowly" or "Take a deep breath before you speak."

5. Be patient and don't worry.

Creating a Learning Environment

Parents may not be able to speed up the acquisition of language, but they can help their children develop a richer vocabulary, a love of communication, and skill as a speaker.

The best way to help your child become a good speaker is to talk. Up until age three, children base most of what they say on the speech of their parents or the adults around them. After that, the language of their peers becomes increasingly important.

When you talk to your child, don't just name objects and expect the words to be learned. Children need to hear words repeatedly, to have the words used in sentences, and to have the words relate closely to objects and experiences important to them. For example, two-year-olds can relate the word *car* to their daily lives. Most won't be able to do this with the word *hydrofoil.*

Talking to your child, however, while necessary is not sufficient in helping him become a good speaker. You must also become an expert listener. Children learn to talk from having one-on-one conversations with adults. Language expert Breyne A. Moskowitz describes a child whose deaf parents used sign language. The child, who had little contact with nondeaf people, was exposed to a daily diet of television viewing. At three, the child was an expert signer but unable to speak or understand English. Don't use television as a means of teaching speech. There has to be an interaction between speaker and listener for your child to develop excellent speaking skills.

The great baby talk controversy

"See the choo-choo." "Tummy hurts." "Did you get a boo-boo?" Is baby talk helpful or harmful? Believe it or not, many experts are beginning to say it is helpful.

Baby talk is made up of simplified words for things such as food and bodily functions, expressed in short, simple sentences spoken in a higher pitch with exaggerated intonation. Before children say their first word, parents may speak in longer, more complex sentences. As soon as children say something understandable, parents simplify their speech. Baby talk is affectionate speech. Its higher pitch and intonation capture children's attention. Most important, it presents a less complicated system of grammar that allows children to figure out how language should be used. Baby talk gives children a simple language that they can imitate.

A cautionary note: The danger with baby talk lies in continuing to use it when a child needs more complex language and a larger vocabulary. A five-year-old shouldn't be hearing "horsie" for "horse" or "bunny wunny" for "rabbit." Nor should he hear, "Look at the doggie. Nice doggie go bow-wow."

To correct or not to correct

"My tooths hurt." "I goed fast." Such grammatical errors grate on parents' nerves. The temptation is to correct these errors. But it is a wasted effort to correct preschool children's grammar. You can model the correct form, but they won't use it until they have figured out the actual rule of grammar behind the form. Because children develop their own simplified rules of grammar, it makes sense to them that plurals are always formed by adding *s* (tooths) and the past tense is always formed by adding *ed* (goed), since in most cases those are the rules. When children discover that there are exceptions to their personal grammar rules, they start using the correct forms.

In addition to being worthless, constant correction can be dangerous. It puts the emphasis on how children speak rather than on what they are saying, which is more important. Children may become increasingly inhibited about expressing themselves for fear of doing it incorrectly.

Activities for You and Your Child

Whenever you choose an activity to do with your child, make sure it is one he will enjoy. It is important for him to have the idea that talking is fun. Be careful not to become a language teacher, focusing all your attention on your child's grammar and vocabulary.

From birth to 15 months

Listening to one-sided conversations. Talk to your baby, especially at diaper-changing, dressing, and feeding times. Tell the child over and over what you are doing. Infants won't understand a word you say but will love the sound of your voice and will get the idea that communication is fun.

Identifying others. Help your child learn names by saying, "Mama is here" or "Daddy is here." Also, be sure to use siblings' names when they are near.

Identifying objects. When you hand your child a rattle, spoon, or any object, always name it. Say, "Here's your rattle" rather than "Here it is."

Identifying specific actions. When you pick your baby up, put him down, or leave the room, always describe your action. "Up you go, baby." "I'm putting you down." "Bye-bye."

Playing an interactive game. Your child can be lying down or sitting facing you for this game. Gently touch foreheads and say, "Ga-Boom" or some other nonsense word. Then smile at your baby to show him that the game is fun. After playing the game several times, your child will smile back at you. Eventually, he will move forward to meet you when you ask if he wants to play Ga-Boom.

From 15 months to 2½ years

Imitating sounds. Having fun imitating sounds encourages children to imitate words. Imitate sounds such as ticking clocks, vacuum cleaners, sirens, and trains, and your child will soon enjoy doing it, too.

Defining words. Help your child define words that he can say by asking questions such as these:

- Do you eat with a fork or ball?

- Do you see with your tummy or your eyes?

- Do you sleep in a bed or a bathtub?

Pantomiming actions. Pantomime actions that your child can describe with words: jumping, hopping, running, crying, and laughing. Make sure the child knows the word for the action.

Reading. Find stories that interest your child and capture his imagination. This will give him a better idea of how to relate his own experiences. Help him learn words by reading stories that repeat words and phrases, such as *Are You My Mother?* by P. D. Eastman. And read favorite stories frequently so that you and your child can chant certain key lines together.

Playing pretend games. Join with your child in pretending to be bus driver and rider, customer and clerk, or any people the child commonly encounters. As your child becomes older, your pretend games can become more imaginative. You can be king and queen, storybook characters, or talking animals.

Taking turns conversing. Build a block tower with your child. Take turns adding blocks, and each time a block is added, say, "My block." You can do the same thing while rolling a ball back and forth with your child.

Repeating favorite nursery rhymes. Expose your child to classic nursery rhymes such as "Jack Sprat," "Mary Had a Little Lamb," and "Jack and Jill" by reciting them frequently. Encourage your child to repeat lines with you while learning them. Make nursery-rhyme time more fun by adding actions. Jack can fall down and so can Humpty Dumpty.

From 2½ years to 5 years

Having a talkative playmate. Give your child the opportunity to play one-on-one with a very verbal child. It will increase your child's desire to communicate.

Answering questions. Stimulate your child's conversational skills by asking questions that require more than a yes or no answer. For example, don't ask, "Do you want to stay home?" Ask instead, "Do you want to stay home or go to the park?" Don't ask, "Do you want to hear Jack and the Beanstalk?" Ask instead, "Which story shall I read tonight?"

Playing giving directions games. Give your child a small object to hide from you in a room. Then have the child tell you whether you are close to finding the object by using phrases such as "You're hot," "You're really hot," or "You're very, very cold." (Hot denotes being close to the object and cold, far away.) In a similar game, have your child hide an object in another room. Then have him give you instructions one at a time until you find the object. An older child could give two- or three-part directions before you start searching for the object.

In another game, best played outdoors or in a playroom, the child who is "It" gives directions to other children. Children are asked to crawl under a table, hop around a tree, or sit in a chair. It is similar to having the children run an obstacle course.

Describing the events of the day. Make the evening meal a time in which each family member tells about what he or she did during the day. At first, it will probably be necessary to ask questions to guide your child's description. Don't expect a long narrative, but do encourage your child to tell at least one thing he did in the morning and one thing he did in the afternoon, which encourages sequencing of events.

Varying intensity and tone of voice. Read a story such as *Goldilocks and the Three Bears* to your child, changing your voice to reflect the personalities of the characters. When your child becomes familiar with a story, have him dramatize lines such as Papa Bear's "Who's been eating my porridge?"

Describing objects. Let your child be "It" and describe an object by giving just one clue at a time. Each player has one chance to guess the object before It gives another clue.

Learning to sequence events. After a visit to an interesting place such as a museum or a new friend's home, suggest that your child help you create a story describing the experience. Encourage him to tell what happened from beginning to end. Write down what your child tells you. If he doesn't know exactly what to say, prompt him with questions such as, "What did you do or see first?" "Why did you like doing that?" Your child can also draw illustrations for the story. Be sure to read the story aloud when you are done and frequently thereafter.

Preparing for show-and-tell. Start by talking with your child about a favorite toy. Ask him to describe its physical characteristics: size, shape, texture, and color. Then have him describe what, if anything, the toy does or how to play with it. Finally, have him explain why the toy is a favorite.

After your child can talk about a toy, choose some common household object and ask your child to describe how it works. The child should be able to explain the step-by-step operation of the object to you. Good choices include telephones, radios, television sets, blenders, and vacuum cleaners.

Starting a scrapbook. Show your child his baby book with its souvenirs of his birth and first year. Obtain a scrapbook that you and your child can use to keep a record of more recent events. Together, you can glue photos, pictures, and other souvenir items in the book. Take time frequently to discuss the experiences suggested by the souvenirs. This activity helps your child see the difference between present and past events.

Above All Else

Don't try to be a teacher of words. It won't work. Instead, be a provider of experiences that elicit conversation. Give your child the idea that talking is fun. And remember that children learn to talk through one-on-one conversations with adults. So, turn the humdrum as well as the exciting events in your child's life into opportunities to talk with him. Let his interests guide most of the dialogue. Few young children want a steady diet of conversation about the economy, planets, or pollution.

Chapter Nine

READING READINESS

On the first day of kindergarten, your child is not going to be asked to sit down and read *Cinderella* to the class. Most kindergartens don't even teach children how to read. Instead, they help children learn the skills that they need to begin reading. And this is what parents should be doing—getting their children ready to read, which simply means getting them excited about and interested in reading. There is no question that reading is the most important skill your child must acquire to be successful in school. The entire curriculum is based on reading. Your child has to be able to read to handle story problems in math; understand maps in geography; and cope with history, science, English, and health. Reading is a skill that is needed not only for school but for every facet of an individual's life, from work to recreational activities.

What Children Need to Learn

Many parents wrongly believe that in order to be ready to read, their child must be able to say and write the alphabet, sound out words, and read a few hundred words. This belief is totally inaccurate and leads to preschoolers laboriously tracing letters and doing endless pages in workbooks, trying to match the *b* sound to ball and the *c* sound to cat. Worst of all, parents' eagerness to help their children become readers can turn children away from the joy of reading. Make sure your child has the proper reading readiness skills:

- good listening skills

- oral language ability

- an understanding of the relationship between spoken and written words

- knowledge of the conventions of print and books

- an eagerness to read

Children who have been read to from infancy know the joy books bring and are well on their way to developing the prereading skills needed for kindergarten. Use the checklist on page 76 to determine your child's progress in acquiring these skills.

How Children Acquire Reading Readiness Skills

Reading readiness is total body readiness. It may seem that the skills required to grasp a toy or bounce a ball have nothing to do with reading, but fine motor skills allow a child to grasp and turn pages in books, and gross motor skills provide the hand-eye coordination necessary for reading.

Teachers do not want parents to push their preschoolers to learn to read. Each child's rate of development, genetic makeup, and level of interest all play important roles in determining reading readiness. Some children need so little help in learning to read that it seems they are teaching themselves.

Parents are constantly bombarded by the message that the way to help their children become readers is to read to them. Many parents wonder if the benefits are proportionate to all the hoopla. They are. Educators say that children who have been read to learn to read much more easily when formal reading instruction begins.

Watch for Signs of Problems

If you answer yes to any of the questions below, it is possible that your child will need extra time and encouragement, plus special help, in acquiring reading readiness skills.

- Was your baby premature?
- Did your baby require oxygen?
- Did your baby have convulsions?
- Has your child ever had fainting or blackout spells?
- Has your child ever had any trouble seeing?
- Have your child's eyes ever looked crossed?
- Is your child unable to bounce a ball?
- Is your child unable to throw a ball?

Checklist of expected prereading skills

	can easily accomplish	can accomplish with difficulty	cannot accomplish
Birth to 15 months			
Enjoys hearing stories, poems, and rhymes			
Enjoys looking at picture books			
By 2½ years			
Shows preference for certain books			
Enjoys hearing stories, poems, and rhymes			
Retells stories			
Has the beginnings of a personal library			
By 5 years			
Expresses self verbally			
Tells stories			
Looks at pictures and tells stories			
Repeats a sentence of six to eight words			
Answers questions about a short story			
Completes an incomplete sentence with the proper word			
Looks at books and magazines			
Enjoys hearing stories, poems, and rhymes			
Identifies rhyming words			
Knows some beginning sounds			
Makes fine visual discriminations			
Knows what an alphabet letter is			
Identifies some alphabet letters			
Recognizes some common sight words, such as *stop*			
Pretends to read			
Understands print carries a message			
Understands the conventions of print			
Has a personal library			

- Does your child often drop things?
- Does your child trip easily?
- Does your child often run into things?
- Is your child unable to follow simple directions?
- Does your child have a short attention span?
- Is your child unable to say most sounds correctly?
- Does your child turn the television on to a very high volume?
- Does your child sit very close to the television set?
- Is your child highly active?
- Does your child have frequent temper tantrums?
- Is it hard for strangers to understand your child?
- Is your child unable to dress herself?

Creating a Learning Environment

Children learn by imitation. You cannot expect your older child to read newspapers for world news if you turn on the television to get your information. Adults need to serve as models for young children. Children should see their parents reading. They also need to hear stories, poems, or rhymes every day of their lives. It isn't ridiculous to start reading to your child from the day she is born. Try the following activities to help your preschooler become interested in reading:

- Take family trips to the library.
- Provide your child with her own books.
- Share a reading time.
- Listen to your child "read."
- Talk together before, during, and after reading.
- Ask questions about what you have read together, but don't make it a "right or wrong" answer session.
- Know your child's attention span. Don't read beyond it.
- Help your child select books that meet her personal interests.

Helping select books

There are thousands of children's books. Librarians can help you find books that are appropriate for your child's age and interests. Also, look for these excellent guides to children's books:

- Andrea E. Cascardi. *Good Books to Grow On.* New York: Warner Books, 1985.

- Eden Ross Lipson. *The New York Times Parent's Guide to the Best Books for Children.* New York: Random House, 1988.

- Jim Trelease. *The Read-Aloud Handbook.* New York: Penguin Books, 1985.

Activities for You and Your Child

If you go about it right, your child will develop a love for listening to the printed word that will, at the right time, turn into a desire to read independently. The following activities should help you.

From birth to 15 months

Sharing inner books. You may not realize it, but parents come equipped with books inside their heads. You have old stories, past experiences, and even traditional verses all stored in your memory ready to tell without even turning a page. Some parents feel silly acting out "This Little Pig Went to Market," but babies love it, and such activities give them a chance to interact with the spoken word.

This Little Pig Went to Market

(Touch each toe one after another, starting with big toe.)
This little pig went to market.
This little pig stayed home.
This little pig ate roast beef.
This little pig had none.
This little pig cried, "Wee, wee, wee!"
All the way home! (Tickle foot.)

Using talking books. To help reinforce the spoken word, play talking books from the minute your baby comes home. Have grandparents or friends make tapes of their favorite stories and nursery rhymes so that your child has the opportunity to listen and react to the sounds of different human voices.

Listening to songs. Parents with newborn infants have a golden opportunity to sing outside the shower. No matter how badly you sing, your baby will love the sound of your voice. Try to recall and sing some of the old lullabies that your parents sang to you.

Using cloth and board books. Cloth books allow children to turn pages and "read" books. These books give children the opportunity to savor a book without destroying it.

Using appropriate books. For this age level, the best books are those that have simple color illustrations and rhyming sounds.

From 15 months to 2½ years

Starting a personal library. Select inexpensive books that your child can carry around and read. Owning books makes them important to a child.

Using talking books. At this age, children are able to do more than just listen to a story. Show them how they can turn the pages as the story is being read to them. Older children will be able to "read" independently.

Reading. When reading to your child, don't forget that she will have a short attention span. Reading sessions don't need to last long. Try to read to her every day at the same time, selecting a time when she is calm. Naptime and bedtime are usually the best. Give your child a broader understanding of the world outside her home by relating what she reads to the outside world. For example, after you read books about zoo animals, you and your child should plan a trip to the zoo, so she can actually see some of the animals she has read about.

Reading nursery rhymes, poems, and jump-rope jingles. Read nursery rhymes, poems, and jingles to your child to accustom her to hearing similar sounds. Your child may join you in "reading" familiar rhymes.

Using appropriate books. At this age, your child still needs books that have simple illustrations. Now is the time to read picture books, even catalogs, to her. Let her name familiar objects in these books. When she expresses interest in a subject, build on that interest by finding a book about it to read to her.

From 2½ to 5 years

Understanding print stands for words. When you are driving down the street, point out that the red sign with the letters *STOP* says stop. It won't take your child long to find the fast food places. At home, show your child the words *on* and *off* on the television and on different appliances. When you read to your child, run your finger under the words occasionally to show her what words you are reading.

Learning the conventions of reading books. Run your finger under words as you read them to show your child that reading goes from left to right, and then bring your finger back across the page to start another line. Make it clear that books are read from the top of the page to the bottom and from front to back.

Having sharp eyes. Show your child two pictures that are almost identical, and ask her to point out the differences between the pictures. Draw a picture of a man and leave off a leg, or a picture of a house without a door. See if your child can figure out what is missing.

Playing word games. Read your child a familiar story, such as *The Little Red Hen.* As you read the word *hen*, change it to *cat* and see if she picks up your error. If your child corrects you, have her name a story that has a cat in it.

Visiting the library. Take your child to the library every week to select new books to read. Don't use the library just as a place to find books; enroll your child in programs that stimulate an interest in reading.

Learning letters of the alphabet. When your child points to a letter of the alphabet, build upon this interest by telling her the name of the letter. Then let her find the letter in books, on blocks, and on signs. It takes a lot of repetition for a child to learn a letter. Having her describe how the letter is made or tracing it in sand may help her learn it. Try to have your child learn one letter before going on to another. This is also a good time to read alphabet books.

Reading helpful books. Prepare your child for the many "firsts" in life through the printed word. For example, read the child a book about going to the dentist before her first trip to the dentist.

Talking about what you read. Tell your child the title of a book before you begin reading it. Also, show her the author's name and explain that books are written by people. Let her predict what a book will be about. Talk about characters and ask your child's opinion as to why they act as they do. Discuss how each book relates to other books and real-life experiences. Stop in the middle of a new story and ask your child to guess how it will end.

Using appropriate books. At this age, children can be introduced to books with chapters and should be reading wordless books so that they have a chance to tell the whole story. Selected fairy tales are also appropriate for children who are almost ready for school.

Above All Else

Becoming a skilled reader is a journey of many steps. Even if you do nothing more than read to your child every day, you have taken the first step in starting your child on the road to being a good reader. Additional informal teaching, such as pointing out words on signs, identifying rhyming sounds, and naming alphabet letters will increase your child's readiness for the kindergarten reading program. The best way for a child to become an avid reader is to see her parents burying their noses in books.

Chapter Ten

UNDERSTANDING NUMBERS

Parents know that schools consider math important. Almost half of children's time in the early grades is spent studying this subject. So you may have decided to teach your child to count and do a few simple addition problems before he starts kindergarten. Eventually, he will have to be able to do these things. But math education, even in kindergarten, involves far more than handling numbers. It means being able to match, classify, compare, and order objects. It is mastery of these basic math concepts—not being able to count to fifty and add two plus two—that determines how well your child will do in math throughout school.

What Children Need to Learn

Teachers don't expect children to count beyond five or to add even simple combinations such as two plus three before entering kindergarten. They do want children to be able to glance at four or five books, cups, or buttons and know immediately that what they see is a group of four or five objects. Forget about teaching your child to recognize more than five objects; he just isn't ready to do this. More important than helping your child learn to recognize numbers is helping him feel at home with the following four basic concepts:

1. *One-to-one matching of objects.* In school, children will need to match objects in one set with objects in another set. For the preschooler this means learning that everyone at the supper table has a plate and that one shoe is put on each foot.

2. *Classifying objects.* In math, all objects in a group have certain qualities in common. You can have sets of four balls, three dolls, or five candies. Therefore, children should know how to sort fruit into a pile of oranges or apples, as well as how to put forks, knives, and spoons in the appropriate slots in the silverware drawer.

3. *Comparing objects.* Comparison is used in understanding relationships in math. For example, one line is longer than another, and

two triangles have the same area. When children use words such as short and long, more and less, or all and none, they are making math comparisons.

4. *Ordering objects.* Numbers have their place in a sequence. For example, 3 comes after 2 and before 4. Preschoolers need to know that five pennies are more than four pennies. Knowing the pattern of activities in their day helps young children understand the concept of ordering or sequencing objects. (First, they are put in their high chairs, then they eat, then their faces are washed.)

Children's development of math skills is closely tied to the development of their thinking skills. They simply can't perform some math operations until they reach a certain stage in their mental development. Use the checklist on page 84 to evaluate your child's progress in acquiring the skills necessary to understand math.

How Children Learn Math Skills

Math is far more than numbers. Children must learn about the relationships between objects before they are ready to work with numbers. Children start on this task within a few weeks of birth when they use their senses to investigate objects. Eventually, they are able to relate past observations to present ones. A child recognizes a new ball as a ball because it looks and behaves like all other balls the child has explored. The child classifies the new object as a ball. With more and more experiences, children build more complex relationships. These classification patterns are the start of mathematical thought. Children must build these patterns by themselves, but parents can help by providing an environment that allows the child to explore a wide variety of objects.

From 2 to 3 years

Once children have begun to talk, they can find out more about objects by asking questions. At this point, parents need to encourage children to describe objects so that different properties such as size and shape can be recognized and comparisons can be made. Parents should expect their child to make many mistakes in comparison activities until he is older. For example, children often say one object is bigger than another because it is taller and will continue to do so

Checklist of expected math skills

	can easily accomplish	can accomplish with difficulty	cannot accomplish

Birth to 15 months

	can easily accomplish	can accomplish with difficulty	cannot accomplish
Judges the distance of an object from self correctly			
Uses all five senses to explore objects			
Identifies an object from different viewpoints			
Sees similarities in some objects			
Is aware that certain events regularly occur after others			

By 2½ years

Uses senses to gain information about objects			
Describes properties of objects (color, shape)			
Sees similarities and differences in objects			
Compares objects by size (big, little)			
Understands objects can be put in order (big, bigger)			
Understands events can be sequenced			
Begins to count objects in sequence (one ball, two balls)			

By 5 years

Recognizes likenesses and differences in shapes			
Sorts similar objects by color, size, and shape			
Matches objects based on shape			
Recognizes circles, squares, and triangles			
Copies simple shapes (circle, square, triangle)			
Understands concept of longest and shortest			
Understands concept of more and less			
Knows position words such as on, behind, under			
Counts objects in sequence to five (one ball, two balls)			
Recognizes groups of one to five objects			
Counts to five			
Arranges blocks in order by size			

until they reach a certain stage in the development of their thinking skills. During the two's and three's, children increase their awareness of new relationships. Now a new ball isn't just a ball, but also a toy. They also develop some number concepts and learn to count in sequence: one ball, two balls, and so on. Children will definitely know the difference between having one or two cookies.

From 4 to 5 years

By five, most children will be able to look at a group of five objects and use the number five for the group. Once this happens, parents can teach the numerals if a child wants to learn them. Most four- and five-year-olds can also match equal sets of numbers. If you put out a row of five red chips, they will be able to match it with another row of five more red chips. If you lay out two equal rows of chips, children this age will readily agree that both rows have the same number of chips. But if you lay out rows of the same number of chips and one row is longer, most children will say that the longer row has more chips. Try this activity with your child.

Children decide that the longer row has more chips because of what they see—not by counting. They will not be able to understand that a quantity remains the same with changed spacing until they are about seven years old. Children can be taught that the rows have equal numbers of chips, but there isn't much point in teaching this because they aren't ready to understand the concept.

Creating a Learning Environment

Few parents can resist teaching their children to count. The idea has merit, too, because teachers want children entering kindergarten to be able to count to five. The best way to teach your child to count is to use objects. Teach your child that a group of three objects, for example, has more objects than a group of two objects. Counting becomes a meaningful exercise rather than something a well-trained parrot could do. Blocks, colored cubes, nesting cups, and beads should be in every home for children to use in matching, classifying, comparing, and ordering. Children also need puzzles, sand, clay, water, and containers to investigate numerical relationships.

Be aware that most preschoolers are unable to attach a number to groups of over five objects. Therefore a child who can count to twenty really has no idea of the difference between ten cents and fifteen cents. Whatever you do, don't bring math workbooks into your home. Children don't learn number concepts by working with numbers on a page, but by handling objects. Workbooks just teach children how to draw lines or fill in the right box to please their parents. Remember that preschool children haven't reached the stage in their thinking skills in which numbers on a page have any real meaning to them. They can be taught that five plus three equals eight, but they won't really understand what it means.

Activities for You and Your Child

Children start out thinking that math is fun. They easily absorb basic math concepts by manipulating objects. But in the elementary grades, many children are turned off by math because they aren't ready to handle the work. The following activities are appropriate ways to develop the basic math concepts needed for school without scaring a child off the subject.

From birth to 15 months

Judging the distance. Put toys within the reach of your infant, placing them at different distances from him. This will help your child learn how to judge distances.

Using the five senses to explore objects. Choose toys for your child that can be explored through several senses, rather than only one or two. A toy that squeaks can be seen, touched, manipulated to make a sound, and heard.

Seeing similarities. Have your child study just two or three toys that are similar, such as two balls of different sizes, three furry toys, or large and small blocks. Allow your child to focus on the similarities of these objects by not having other toys or distractions around.

From 15 months to 2½ years

Matching objects. Reading *Goldilocks and the Three Bears* to your child will reinforce the idea of one-to-one correspondence because each bear has his or her own porridge, chair, and bed. Having your child and a few friends play Musical Chairs (for directions see page 44) with the same number of chairs as children will also strengthen the idea of one-to-one correspondence.

Playing Lotto with your child, using very simple cards, will give your child practice in matching objects. Each player has a Lotto card with six or eight pictures. Players take turns drawing from the deck of cards. If the card matches a player's picture, the card is placed over the picture. The winner is the first to cover his Lotto card. You can buy or make Lotto games.

Classifying objects. At this age, children should be classifying objects by only one property. Try the following activities:

1. Have your child find all the towels or handkerchiefs in the laundry, all the spoons in the dishwasher holder, all the cans in the grocery bags, or all the potatoes in the vegetable bin.

2. Give your child poker chips of two colors, red and black checkers, or beads of two colors, and ask him to sort the chips, checkers, or beads into two piles by color.

3. Gather several of your child's toys. Then have him make a pile of all the toys that have wheels, all the toys that bounce, or all the toys that are red.

Comparing objects. Teach size comparison by frequently describing one object as bigger or smaller than another. Then put small plastic animals or cars in a bag, and have your child draw out two objects at a time, telling which is bigger or smaller.

Counting numbers. To have your child become familiar with number words, recite nursery rhymes such as "One, Two, Buckle My Shoe" or "One, Two, Three, Four, Five."

One, Two, Buckle My Shoe

One, two, buckle my shoe.
Three, four, shut the door.
Five, six, pick up sticks.
Seven, eight, lay them straight.
Nine, ten, a big fat hen.

One, Two, Three, Four, Five

One, two, three, four, five,
Once I caught a fish alive.
Six, seven, eight, nine, ten,
Then I let it go again.
Why did you let it go?
Because it bit my finger so.
Which finger did it bite?
The little finger on the right.

From 2½ to 5 years

Matching objects. One of the easiest ways for children to gain skill in one-to-one correspondence is through setting the table. Each place at the table has one napkin, one plate, one glass, one fork, one knife, and one spoon. You can use other activities to practice this skill:

1. Give your child a checkerboard and checkers. Have your child put all the red checkers on red squares and all the black checkers on black squares.

2. When baking cookies, have your child place one raisin, nut, or candy on each cookie ready to go in the oven.

3. Make a grid and have your child put one coin, poker chip, or bead in each square.

Classifying objects. Once children have become skilled at classifying objects by one property, they can try classifying more objects, handling more difficult classifications, or classifying a group of objects in more than one way.

1. Give your child several small waterproof objects and a pan of water. Have the child test whether an object will float and put it into a "float" or "not float" pile.

2. Stack a pile of toys in front of your child. Have the child sort the toys into piles of wooden or plastic toys.

3. Cut pictures of objects from magazines, and have your child put them into piles of things used indoors or outdoors.

4. Have your child sort beads by color and then by size.

5. Give your child pictures from a magazine or a jar of buttons, assorted coins, or beads and ask the child to sort these objects into groups using his own classification system.

Comparing objects. After you put a number of small toys or familiar objects in a bag, have your child draw two objects at a time from the bag and tell how the objects are similar. Use the same objects another day, asking the child to tell how the objects are different. You may have to give clues to help younger children make these comparisons.

It is usually enough to ask if the objects are the same color, size, or shape. Turn over all the dominoes in a set. Have your child draw one of the dominoes and tell you which end has more dots. Ask the child to continue until ten dominoes have been compared.

Counting numbers. Through playing a wide variety of games, children can practice counting numbers.

1. Board games such as Candyland and Chutes and Ladders involve counting spaces to reach a goal. In some of these games, cards that force a child to go back several spaces can be removed to make the game move faster and avoid the child's distress at moving a marker backward. In addition, you can remove high number cards or use only one die to make a simpler game for young children.

2. Make several grids. Then have players throw a die and put as many pennies on their grid as the number on the die. Players alternate turns until one has filled each space on his grid with a penny.

3. Your child can play Concentration alone or with another player (at first, he can use just the face cards and the numbers he knows in the deck of cards): The cards are placed face down in rows, and the players turn over two cards each turn. If a match is made, the cards are removed and the player has another turn. If not, the cards are placed face down again.

4. The card game War can be played with a homemade deck of cards: Make four cards for each number from one through five, and put the appropriate number of dots on each card. All the cards are dealt, and the two players lay down their top cards face up. The player who has the greater number of dots on his card picks up both cards. If the cards have the same number of dots, two more cards are laid face down. Each player turns his top card face up, and the player whose card has more dots picks up all the cards. The winner is the player who has captured all of the cards. Because this game can last a long time, it is a good idea to set a time limit. Older children will enjoy playing this game with a deck that has numbers instead of dots.

Attaching meaning to numbers. Your child will need considerable practice in learning what the names of numbers mean.

- Develop understanding of the number two by having your child find the parts of his body that come in twos.

- Practice attaching meaning to numbers by asking your child for one pencil, two apples, three cups, and so on.

- Select three buttons, coins, blocks, or beads. Then hide one, two, or three of these objects under a piece of cardboard. Quickly raise the cardboard, and let your child glance at the objects for a second. Ask him to tell you how many objects there are. If he is correct, hide a different number of objects. If he is incorrect, show the objects again. Do not let the child see the objects long enough to count them: You want the child to associate the numbers with the objects automatically. As your child's ability grows, increase the number of objects to four and then five.

Learning numerals. Before children start to write numerals, they need to become familiar with how numbers look.

- Make a number book with your child for the numbers one through five. Write one numeral on each page, and have the child draw the appropriate number of objects (dots, balls, or squares) for each number.

- Read number books with your child, drawing the child's attention to the written numbers as you read about them.

- Play Bingo with your child with a homemade set of Bingo cards. Instead of writing *BINGO* at the top of each player's card, draw dots of five different colors and fill the three spaces under each colored dot with a number between one and five. Make a set of cards for the caller too. On each of the caller's cards, draw one color dot and one number. The caller draws a card and calls out the number and color, such as "red two" or "green five." Players having this combination cover it with a marker. The winner is the first player to have all spaces covered vertically or horizontally.

- Play a game with your child using a deck that has the numerals one through five on half of the cards and dots or pictures representing those numbers on the rest of the cards. All of the cards are dealt. The players take turns trying to match the numeral cards with the equivalent dot or picture cards by asking another player questions such as, "Do you have a five?" The other player has to provide such a card if he has it. The winner is the first to match all of his cards.

Writing numerals. Children shouldn't have to learn to write the numerals one to five by tracing them in workbooks. Try using the following activities:

• Cut out sandpaper numerals for your child to trace with his fingers before he attempts to write numerals.

• Trace a numeral in sand, and let your child deepen the pattern.

• Write large numerals on a chalkboard or marker board for your child to trace.

• Have your child write numerals on a chalkboard or marker board before attempting to write them on paper.

Above All Else

Remember, it is not counting and writing numbers that make a child ready to handle math in school; it is understanding the basic concepts of math. Don't try to teach these concepts directly. Instead, provide fun experiences that will help your child discover the concepts for himself.

Chapter Eleven

HOP, SKIP, AND CATCH

Remember that Carl Lewis, the Olympic gold medalist in track and field, was not born running. Your child may never run as fast as Carl, but speed isn't important. What's important is learning how to control the large muscles in the legs, arms, and neck in order to be able to run, jump, skip, hop, climb, and ride a bicycle. The use, control, and coordination of these muscles are known as gross motor skills. Gross motor skills give children the movement that lets them explore their environment.

In school, gross motor skills are important in the classroom as well as on the playground. Children have to be able to look quickly and without thinking from their papers to the teacher or the chalkboard, or they won't be able to pay full attention to what is being taught in the classroom. Furthermore, the small muscles used for writing are closely related to the large muscles that will get the hand into the correct position for writing.

What Children Need to Learn

To master gross motor skills, children have to learn how to move their bodies. More important, they have to learn how to move their bodies without thinking about it. For example, a child should be able to raise a hand immediately when the teacher says, "Raise your hand if you brought something for show-and-tell." When playing games, a child should be able to jump, hop on one foot, or skip with ease. Children also have to distinguish left from right, move both sides of their bodies, and develop a sense of balance—a prerequisite for mastering most gross motor skills.

Before you help improve your child's gross motor skills, use the checklist on pages 94–95 to see how many of these skills your child has acquired. Rate a skill as "can easily accomplish" if your child can do it with flowing movements and no hesitation.

How Children Learn Gross Motor Skills

The old adage "You have to crawl before you walk" is not necessarily true. Gross motor development is different in every individual. Some babies walk without going through the crawling stage. One baby may only be starting to crawl at ten months while another of the same age may be tearing around the house.

Some children are natural athletes who quickly catch on to skipping and throwing balls, and others need considerable practice to acquire large muscle skills. And, as all adults know, even with great amounts of practice there are some muscle movements that are never completely mastered. Just ask any golfer, bowler, or tennis player.

Body control proceeds from head to toe and then from trunk to extremities. Babies first learn to hold up, control, and move their heads and then their necks, arms, legs, fingers, and toes.

Watch for Signs of Problems

No two children develop gross motor skills at the same rate. But medical experts have been able to gauge "normal" stages of growth for different age groups. You can use the following "developmental milestones" from the American Academy of Pediatrics as guidelines to judge when something might be wrong and help is needed.

Observe your child over a one-month period when you apply any of the milestones. This will allow you to take into account any days when your child is upset or under stress. Remember, failing to meet a milestone does not necessarily mean that your child has a problem with gross motor development.

Plan to talk to your child's pediatrician during your next office visit if you note or suspect any major changes from the following milestones or the child does not do many of the things suitable for her age.

3 months

• When lying on her back, your child can move each of her arms and legs equally well.

• When you hold your child in the standing position, she can support her head for more than a moment.

• Your child has rolled over at least two times from her stomach to her back or her back to her stomach.

Checklist of expected gross motor skills

	can easily accomplish	can accomplish with difficulty	cannot accomplish
Birth to 15 months			
Lifts head			
Holds head up			
Sits without help			
Rolls over			
Crawls			
Crawls upstairs			
Crawls downstairs backward			
Pulls up to a standing position			
Balances on two feet			
Stands alone			
Takes a step			
Walks			
Walks and pushes an object			
Walks and carries a toy			
Throws an object			
By 2½ years			
Walks on uneven surfaces			
Walks backward			
Walks upstairs using both feet and relying on support			
Climbs			
Starts to run			
Jumps off one step			
Rides small toy by pushing with feet			
Sits alone in a small chair			
Catches a ball			
Rolls a ball			
Pulls an object			
Copies simple movements			

	can easily accomplish	can accomplish with difficulty	cannot accomplish
By 5 years			
Bends			
Walks a straight line			
Walks sideways			
Walks up and down stairs alternating feet			
Stands on tiptoes			
Walks on tiptoes			
Walks on a low balance beam			
Marches			
Runs			
Jumps forward			
Jumps continuously			
Jumps backward			
Jumps and lands on both feet in one spot			
Jumps rope			
Skips			
Gallops			
Leaps			
Hops			
Stands on one foot with eyes open for 5 seconds			
Stands on one foot with eyes closed			
Drops and catches a ball			
Bounces a ball			
Kicks a ball			
Swings			
Pedals a tricycle or bicycle			

• When you hold your child under her arms, she tries to stand on her feet and support some of her weight on her legs.

12 months
• Your child crawls on hands and knees.

• Your child pulls up to stand.

• Your child walks holding on to furniture.

18 months
• Your child can walk all the way across a large room without falling or wobbling from side to side.

• Your child can walk without support or help.

2 years
• Your child can run without falling.

3 years
• Your child can throw a ball overhand (not sidearm or underhand) toward your stomach or chest from a distance of five feet.

4 years
• Your child can pedal a tricycle at least ten feet forward.

5 years
• Your child can walk down stairs alternating feet.

• Your child can broad jump.

Source: Adapted with permission from "Your Child's Growth: Developmental Milestones." © 1990 American Academy of Pediatrics.

Creating a Learning Environment

Your goal as a parent is not to speed up your child's large muscle development but to make sure that your child has opportunities to develop and practice using these muscles. For most children, it is enough just to do the things they love: pushing and pulling toys, running, jumping, swinging, and riding tricycles. Don't let your child be a couch potato who is content to sit and watch television all day. Instead, encourage her to be active by providing these playthings:

- a balance beam
- balls
- beanbags
- climbing equipment
- a jump rope
- a jungle gym
- large boxes

- open space
- push-pull toys
- riding toys without pedals
- a slide
- a swing
- a tricycle
- a wading pool

Activities for You and Your Child

Infants, toddlers, and preschoolers enjoy physical activity. Besides helping them gain gross motor skills, activity also gives them an opportunity to explore their environment. The toddler is able to investigate far more of the world than the child who hasn't yet learned to walk. While children use their large muscles, they learn about how things relate in space: near and far, up and down, in and out. Use the following activities to guide you in planning for your child's large muscle development.

From birth to 15 months

Exercising arms and legs. Although infants usually get enough exercise, most enjoy brief exercise sessions with their parents. Limit these times to no more than five minutes because infants tire easily.

Place your child on her back on the floor for these exercises. Tell her what you are going to do. Begin by putting one of your fingers in each of the infant's hands. Next, slowly extend her arms, being careful not to pull her head or body off the floor. Then shake one arm lightly. You will know that your child is relaxing when her hands relax. When you exercise your child's legs, massage lightly, starting at the toes and working up the leg. Carefully hold the leg, supporting the whole knee, and slowly bend the knee up toward the chest. Be careful not to push the legs up too far. You can also raise and lower your baby's legs.

Doing lift ups. This activity should only be done after your baby has good head control. Turn on some music and then sit in a chair with your child facing you. Hold her firmly under the arms, and slowly lift her off your lap. Gently bounce her up and down as you listen to the music. This activity will help strengthen your baby's coordination and leg muscles.

Rolling. As early as six weeks, a baby may be rolling from back to stomach; however, some six-month-old babies are still struggling to roll over. Interest your baby in rolling over by placing her on the floor with a fascinating toy on one side. Grasp the underside of the baby's leg on the side that you want her to roll toward. Move your hand up to her buttocks and, at the same time, extend the baby's opposite arm alongside her head. With this help, the baby should roll over. Remember to talk to your baby about what you are doing throughout the activity.

Pulling up. Place your baby in a kneeling position facing the bars in her crib. Put the baby's fingers around the bars and gently help her hands move up the bars. When the baby is almost standing, put her hands on the railing. When your baby is fully standing, let go—but have your hands through the bars to catch her, if necessary. If your baby's legs give way, it is too early to start this exercise.

Playing Catch Me. Crawl beside your baby, and then let her crawl ahead. Wait a few seconds, and crawl after her. Say, "Here I come to get you." When you get to your baby, give her a hug. Then let her start off again.

From 15 months to 2½ years

Rolling and throwing. When your child throws a ball to you, pick it up and roll it back. Throw the ball yourself, and have the child roll it back.

Kicking the ball. Use a large cardboard box or an empty laundry basket as a target. Put a ball several feet from the target and gently kick the ball inside. Have your child do the same thing. The distance can be changed as your child becomes more adept at making goals.

Following a path. Trace your child's feet. Then cut out several pairs of these feet. Arrange them in a path for your child to follow. You can do this activity in the basement or outside on cement. If you use contact paper, the same path can be followed more than once.

Playing Simon Says. Play Simon Says (for directions see page 17), directing your child and others in activities using their large muscles.

They can bend, stretch, hop, jump, or do acrobatics. Increase the difficulty of the movements to meet your child's ever-increasing skill level.

Running an obstacle course. Make an obstacle course with cardboard-box tunnels to crawl through, boxes and footstools to climb over, a ladder laid on the ground to walk through, a small slide, and a string circle to hop in and out of. Vary the course to keep your child interested.

Jumping rope. Put a piece of rope or tape down on the ground. Have your child jump across it without stepping on it.

Rolling over. Have your child lie down on the floor, or outside in an open space, and roll over and over (and over and over) again.

Pounding. You can make or buy a pounding table. Start with only a few large wooden pegs for your child to pound into the holes in the pounding table with a wooden hammer. Demonstrate how to hit a peg several times before she tries this activity.

Stacking. Have your child stack large boxes one on top of another to build a tower. This activity encourages her to stand on tiptoes and to reach.

Tossing beanbags. Draw or tape the face of an animal on a box or wastebasket. Ask your child to feed the animal by tossing a beanbag or a tennis ball into its mouth.

From 2½ to 5 years

Kicking and running. Turn your child loose with a ball in an open area. Encourage her to kick the ball, run after it, and kick it again. Join your child in this game—it is more fun if you both try to reach the ball.

Playing Follow the Leader. Start this activity with you as leader (for directions see page 45). Hop like a frog, dance like a ballerina, crawl like a baby, waddle like a duck, and walk a straight line like a tightrope walker. Then have your child be the leader.

Riding a broomstick horse. A broom with a bag over the top can be transportation for a cowboy or for a princess riding to town.

Pretending to be an animal. Name an animal and ask your child to act and sound like that animal. Good pretend animals include snakes, monkeys, frogs, ducks, bees, birds, elephants, and giraffes.

Playing games. Introduce your child to the games that have delighted generations of children: Hopscotch, Hide and Seek, London Bridge, The Farmer in the Dell (for directions see page 44); Duck, Duck, Gray Duck (also known as Duck, Duck, Goose); and any other favorites you remember from your childhood.

Hopscotch

Draw a hopscotch board like the one shown here. Each player takes a turn throwing a penny or rock onto the first block marked "1." If the token lands in the box, the child jumps over the first box onto the box marked "2" and onto boxes "3" and "4," landing with one foot in each box. She must then hop to each consecutive box—on one foot for a single box and two feet for double boxes. When she reaches box "10," she must turn around and go over the board again, avoiding the box with the token in it. At the end of the course, she picks up her token and jumps over its box. If at any time a player steps on a line, misthrows a token, or falls, she must start at the beginning of the game with box "1" on her next turn. The first player to make it across the whole board (up through box "10") without any mistakes is the winner.

```
        10
         9
      7     8
         6
         5
      3     4
         2
         1
```

Hide and Seek

The player who is "It" covers her eyes and counts to fifty (or twenty, depending on the age of the child) at a designated "home base" while all of the other players hide. She must then search for the other players one by one. Each player who is found joins the child who is It and helps seek out the others. During the game, any player who has not been found is allowed to run for home base. The child who is It can chase and tag the runner. If caught, the runner must join the search for the others. At the end of the game, the first child who was found or tagged becomes It.

(This is just one of many versions of this game.)

London Bridge

Two children face each other and join hands high to form a bridge. Each takes the name of something valuable, such as "diamond" and "ruby." The other children begin walking under the bridge one by one, holding hands or clothing, as everyone sings the song. Upon "My fair lady," the bridge lowers its arms to capture a child. The captured child whispers the name of "diamond" or "ruby" and becomes part of the bridge by holding the back of the child with that name. After all the children are captured in this fashion, the diamonds and rubies have a tug of war.

London Bridge is falling down,
Falling down, falling down.
London Bridge is falling down,
My fair lady.

Build it up with wood and clay...
Wood and clay will wash away...
Build it up with bricks and mortar...
Bricks and mortar will wear away...
Build it up with iron and steel...
Iron and steel with bend and bow...
Build it up with silver and gold...
Silver and gold will be stolen away...
Set a man to watch all night...
Suppose a man will fall alseep...
Give him a pipe to smoke all night...
Suppose the pipe should fall and break...
Get a dog to bark all night...
Suppose the dog should meet a bone...
Get a cock to crow all night...
Here's a prisoner I have got...
What's the prisoner done to you...
Stole my hat and lost my keys...
One hundred pounds will set him free...
One hundred pounds he has not got...
Off to prison he must go...

Duck, Duck, Gray Duck

A group of children sits cross-legged in a circle. The first child who is "It" walks around the circle, tapping the heads of the other children and calling out "duck" as she passes each one. The child who is called "gray duck" instead of "duck" must chase It around the circle. The child who is It runs for the empty spot in the circle. If she reaches the spot and sits down before being tagged, the gray duck becomes It. If tagged, the child must be It again.

Moving to music. Investigate the many records that encourage children to exercise their large muscles while listening to songs. Try "Looby Loo," "Here We Go 'Round the Mulberry Bush," and "The Wheels on the Bus." Perform the actions the songs describe.

Looby Loo

Refrain (hold hands and skip in a circle):
Here we go looby loo,
Here we go looby light,
Here we go looby loo,
All on a Saturday night.

You put your right hand in,
You put your right hand out,
You give your hand a shake, shake, shake,
And turn yourself about.

You put your left hand in...
You put your right foot in...
You put your left foot in...
You put your right arm in...
You put your left arm in...
You put your right leg in...
You put your left leg in...
You put your head in...
You put your whole self in...

Here We Go 'Round the Mulberry Bush

Here we go 'round the mulberry bush,
The mulberry bush, the mulberry bush;
Here we go 'round the mulberry bush,
On a cold and frosty morning!

This is the way we wash our clothes,
Wash our clothes, wash our clothes;
This is the way we wash our clothes,
On a cold and frosty morning!

This is the way we dry our clothes...
This is the way we mend our shoes...
This is the way we sweep the floor...
This is the way we brush our hair...
This is the way we go to school...

The Wheels on the Bus

The wheels on the bus go round and round,
Round and round, round and round.
The wheels on the bus go round and round,
All through the town.

The horn on the bus goes beep, beep, beep...
The wipers on the bus go swish, swish, swish...
The people on the bus go up and down...

The children on the bus make too much noise...
The mothers on the bus go shh, shh, shh...
The babies on the bus fall fast asleep...

Bowling. Use oatmeal boxes or milk cartons and a ball. Stand the boxes up, and then show your child how to roll the ball to knock them down.

Throwing balls. Have your child collect all her balls. Then have her throw them from the same spot, collect the balls, and throw them again and again.

Marching to a tune. Play a stirring march and get your child marching. Then stop the record. Have the child stop marching until you start the record again. Be patient: it takes a while for children to catch on to this.

Pushing. Have your child lie on her back on the floor. Place your hands on her feet, pushing against them until her knees rest against the chest. Then have your child try to push away from you by straightening her legs.

Acting like a pinwheel. Use a piece of string to form a circle on the floor about 1 foot in diameter. Have your child lie down on the floor with her head in the circle. Her head is to stay in the circle as her body moves in a large circle around it. Try this both clockwise and counterclockwise.

Playing. Leave time in your child's day for free play. She can dig in the garden, swing, slide, climb, and run.

Above All Else

Most children automatically and happily develop good gross motor skills through their daily activities. If your child lags in the development of these skills, give her the chance to catch up with her peers by initiating and participating in physical activities with your child. No child wants to be considered a klutz by peers.

Chapter Twelve

WHAT ABOUT PRESCHOOL?

Children are starting school sooner than ever before. Today, about 50 percent of all four-year-olds are in some kind of school program where they spend half days in structured socialization and enrichment experiences. Because more women are working and need full-day child care, some preschools now have two half-day preschool sessions or preschool in the morning and child care in the afternoon. Will going to preschool give your child an advantage over those who remain at home? Not necessarily. Whether at school or at home, the best education for young children occurs in a warm and caring environment that provides them with a variety of new experiences.

The Value of Preschool

Preschool programs do have value. They can help parents provide their children with the rich background of experiences necessary for success in school. Preschools can offer your child these benefits:

- *Training in social skills.* Through playing with other children, a child picks up the skills of sharing, negotiating, and cooperating and gains experience in forming friendships.

- *An awareness of others' feelings.* A child learns that others share his worries, fears, and delights—a first step in realizing such feelings are not unique to him alone.

- *A greater trust in adults.* By finding out that other adults will care for him, a child learns that he can trust adults other than his parents, which makes the world feel like a safer place.

- *A greater sense of independence.* At home a child receives a great deal of one-on-one attention from his parents. At school the teacher's attention must be shared with others, making the child more self-reliant.

- *Improved listening and speaking skills.* A child has to develop these skills to communicate successfully with the teacher and other children.

- *New experiences.* From trips to a bakery to new songs and dances, a child is introduced to activities that help him learn more about the world.

- *Stimulation and activity.* A child gets to play with a variety of equipment and materials in a place primarily designed for play.

- *Increased self-esteem.* By succeeding at school tasks, a child becomes more confident of his abilities.

- *The satisfaction of belonging to a group.* A child gains a sense of security by learning how to participate with others in school activities.

- *An easier transition to kindergarten.* A child gains an appreciation of what school is like and develops a positive attitude toward school. He also becomes more comfortable with being away from home for part of the day.

The Disadvantages of Preschool

Preschool is not for every child. Some children can't handle the separation from their parents while others may not have developed the necessary social skills. Forcing an extremely reluctant child to attend preschool could be damaging to the child's future attitude toward school.

Few children, however, immediately feel at home in a preschool setting. Give your child several weeks to adjust to preschool. During that period first-day fears and problems may disappear. If the child is still not comfortable after that time, you should consider withdrawing him from the program.

Attending preschool can also turn children off from school if the program is not well run or the teachers lack expertise in handling young children. Too strict or too permissive teachers can cause children to develop a strong dislike for school.

Choosing a Preschool

If you decide to send your child to preschool, the next step is finding the right one. Examine the following:

- *Accreditation.* High quality preschools throughout the country are accredited by the National Association for the Education of Young Children (NAEYC). Some of these schools may be in your area.

- *Curriculum.* Avoid schools that teach reading or math in a formal way and that concentrate on academics. Remember that parrots can be taught to count and monkeys to recognize letters. Find a program that will help your child develop socially, emotionally, physically, and intellectually. Make sure that your child will be able to choose from a variety of interesting hands-on activities that the teachers have set up in the play area. Do not enroll your child in a program where all activities are directed by the teacher.

- *Child-adult ratio.* The NAEYC recommends that two- and three-year-olds be in groups of no more than fourteen with at least two adults. For four- and five-year-olds, two adults can handle groups of twenty children.

- *Physical layout.* Look for a roomy, clean place with well-organized play materials that the children can easily reach. You should find areas for playing with blocks, housekeeping, doing artwork, and just sitting and daydreaming. There should be lots of hands-on materials, such as wood, sand, water, and clay. The playground should have safe, sturdy equipment. The NAEYC recommends at least thirty-five square feet of usable playroom floor space indoors for each child and seventy-five square feet of play space outdoors per child.

- *Teachers.* The most important factor in selecting a preschool is the quality of the teachers. You want to find teachers who are genuinely interested in children, listen carefully to what the children say, talk to them, and make learning exciting.

Visiting the school

Never choose a preschool without visiting it for a few hours *without* your child. Good schools welcome visitors. No school will be perfect, but you will get a sense of whether the environment is right for your child. During your visit make sure you see:

- Children who are eager to participate in activities.

- Teachers who comfort and console children and handle discipline problems in a fair and consistent fashion.

Your child's opinion

Before enrolling your child in a preschool, it is also important to visit the preschool *with* your child. Most children will not feel completely at ease in a strange place with unfamiliar people, but you should be able to sense how your child is reacting to the feel of the place.

Alternatives to Preschool

Remember that half of all young children do not attend preschool. Remaining at home with their families, close relatives, or caregivers can provide these children with the advantage of additional nurturing time. The additional one-on-one contact with adults can also help children further develop their speaking skills and build their vocabularies. To enhance the stay-at-home experience, many parents join with other parents to form play groups that meet in their homes a few times a week. In addition to providing children with playmates, these play groups let children investigate new surroundings, play with different toys, enjoy new experiences, and interact with a variety of caring adults.

Above All Else

Preschool should not be an academic experience. Remember, young children develop intellectually not by handling symbols such as letters and numbers, but by actually handling objects. Send your child to preschool to give him exciting new experiences beyond those you can provide in your home and to let him have fun with other children. Find a school where your child can do puzzles, mold clay, paint, swing, climb, and engage in other traditional preschool activities under the guidance of caring teachers.

Chapter Thirteen

READY OR NOT FOR KINDERGARTEN

Your child is five. She has been raised in a nurturing environment, and you have spent considerable time talking and reading to her. She has played with blocks, puzzles, dolls, and balls. Most of the time, she likes playing with friends, has fun with grandparents or other adults, and feels pretty good about the world. She also knows how to get dressed and handle most personal needs. Is this happy child ready to take on the world and go to kindergarten? Probably, yes!

Is My Child Really Ready?

There is no foolproof way to determine whether your child is ready for kindergarten. No perfect test or checklist exists, although tests and checklists can be useful in making this decision. Nor is there one magic age that guarantees success in school. You may find it helpful to consult with your child's preschool teacher, pediatrician, and others who know the child well in order to evaluate her readiness. Your own opinion is the most important: you are the one who knows your child best.

Considering test scores

It is quite possible that your child will be tested by the local school district before she enters kindergarten. Two types of tests are commonly used:

- *Readiness tests* assess a child's level of preparedness for kindergarten.

- *Screening tests* are used to identify children who may be in need of special services.

Unfortunately, these tests are not consistently accurate. You may or may not receive reliable information about your child's abilities. Young children are generally poor test takers, and the test givers are frequently not qualified to give or score these tests. Moreover, children change so quickly that tests given in the spring may not describe the child who is supposed to enter school in the fall. You will receive the most reliable test information from a readiness test administered individually to your child by a well-qualified test administrator or child psychologist.

Final checklist of kindergarten readiness

This final checklist will assist you in evaluating whether your child has developed the skills she needs to handle kindergarten successfully. Your child should be ready for kindergarten if she:

- ☐ is happy away from home
- ☐ has a good sense of herself as an individual
- ☐ handles personal needs
- ☐ shares with others
- ☐ functions as a member of a group
- ☐ follows two- and three-step directions
- ☐ follows rules
- ☐ maintains attention on adult-directed tasks for short periods of time
- ☐ bounces and catches a ball
- ☐ runs, jumps, skips, hops, marches, and walks on tiptoes
- ☐ knows colors
- ☐ copies simple shapes
- ☐ colors pictures
- ☐ cuts with scissors
- ☐ counts to five
- ☐ recognizes groups of five objects
- ☐ groups objects on the basis of one or more characteristics
- ☐ recognizes similarities and differences in objects
- ☐ understands that material is read from top to bottom and left to right

☐ understands that print carries a message

☐ can tell the meaning of common words

☐ hears the differences between similar sounds

☐ carries on conversations with others

☐ produces understandable speech

☐ retells simple stories in sequence

☐ listens to short stories without interruption

☐ appreciates rhymes, poems, stories, and music

Remember, young children change rapidly. A child who cannot count to five, hop, or copy shapes in May may be able to do those things in July or August before school starts.

Understanding the age effect

Almost every research study on the age of entry to school concludes that the youngest children in kindergarten classes usually do not do as well as the oldest children.

There is disagreement about how long the effects of being youngest last. Kinard and Reinherz* found that differences due to age disappeared by third grade. On the other hand, other researchers, including Peck, McCaig, and Sapp,** found some slight academic difficulty continued throughout the elementary years.

Dealing with the age effect

Currently, states and local school districts are moving back the enrollment dates so that children will be older when they start school. Some schools are also placing the youngest children in junior kindergartens.

Many parents are dealing with the problem of age by keeping their children, especially boys, who would be youngest in their class out of school for a year. They are voluntarily holding their children back in order to give them the advantage of being the oldest in their class.

---

*E.M. Kinard and H. Reinherz. "Birthdate Effects on School Performance and Adjustment: A Longitudinal Study." *Journal of Educational Research* 79 (1986): 366-72.

**J.T. Peck, G. McCaig, and M.E. Sapp. *Kindergarten Policies: What Is Best for Children?* Washington, D.C.: National Association for the Education of Young Children, 1988.

No matter what states, schools, and parents do, there will always be youngest and oldest children in a class. The best solution to this problem lies in parents' demanding that schools provide a curriculum that is appropriate for all children who are eligible to enter school. Until schools do this, parents will continue to delay the entry of their young children into kindergarten.

Making the decision

Don't base a decision on your child's readiness for kindergarten on any one factor. Tests may not accurately describe your child's abilities. Checklists will only tell you whether your child has acquired the skills most schools want the child to have. In considering entry age, remember that being among the oldest in a class does not guarantee success nor does being the youngest mean the child will not succeed.

Above All Else

You want your child to have a successful experience in kindergarten because it will make her feel competent and set the stage for long-term achievement at school. For this reason, it is vital that you make sure your child is ready for kindergarten.

Chapter Fourteen

READY, SET, GO

You have helped prepare your child for kindergarten emotionally, physically, socially, and intellectually because you realize how important that first year in school is. You need to take just a few more practical measures to make sure that your child's first year of school goes smoothly.

Choosing the Right Kindergarten Program

In many school districts, you will be able to select the type of kindergarten program your child attends. You may also have to decide whether a full-day or half-day program is best for him.

Academic versus developmental programs

These are two major and quite different approaches to kindergarten education: *Academic programs* stress the development of intellectual skills through formal instruction, while *developmental programs* are concerned with the development of the whole child. You are most likely to find programs that emphasize one approach and include elements of the other.

Remember, young children learn best from hands-on activities. Avoid programs where your child will have to do a substantial amount of workbook and seated activities and where all children are involved in formal reading instruction. A five-year-old is not ready to be chained to his desk. Choose a program that leaves a major part of the day free for play and child-chosen activities.

Full-day versus half-day programs

Today's kindergarten programs may last a half day, a full day, a full day followed by day care, or a full day on alternate days. The number of children attending full-day programs is growing rapidly. Currently, approximately 40 percent of all kindergartners attend full-day programs.

Studies have shown that kindergartners who attend full-day programs have a more relaxed school experience and also perform better on basic skill tests in the first three grades than those who attend half-day programs. These children also tend to have a better attitude toward school and are less likely to be held back. On the other hand, full-day programs can deprive children who would otherwise be home of nurturing time with their parents—time that could also improve their language and thinking skills through one-on-one interaction with adults. Ultimately, when choosing a kindergarten for your child the most important factor is not the length of the day, but the type of program.

Enrolling Your Child in Kindergarten

Don't wait until the last minute to gather all the information necessary to enroll your child in kindergarten. You will be expected to complete an enrollment card similar to the one on page 116.

You will also need a document such as a birth certificate, passport, baptismal record, or hospital record that verifies your child's birth date.

The school will also expect you to have certain information about your child's medical history. You will need to have an accurate record of your child's immunizations and be ready to complete a chart similar to the one on page 117.

Some schools will require children to have complete physical and dental examinations before enrollment. If these examinations are required at your school, schedule appointments early because they are hard to get during the month of August. Even if it is not required, get a physical exam at this time. Doctors are sometimes able to alert parents to conditions that may interfere with learning.

The registration process

Children are often registered for kindergarten in the spring before the close of school. Check for the dates in your local newspaper or call the school where you plan to enroll your child. In some areas it is important to register your child early in order to obtain a desired school or program, as children may be assigned to schools and programs on a first-come, first-served basis.

As part of the enrollment process, your child may be tested for kindergarten readiness. He will feel more comfortable in the testing situation if you can let him know what to expect. Find out all you can about what the test is like and how it will be administered, and then playact the testing situation with him.

Expect to leave registration with an information packet. Read it carefully. It may help to read the information several times to make sure you understand the curriculum and the policies on attendance, conferences, progress reports, special services, school closings, dress, and discipline. Keep the packet handy so that you will be able to refer to it during the school year.

Safety Is Important

Young children are impulsive. They may know safety rules but forget to follow them. If your child will be walking to school, walk the route with him several times. Review the following safety rules as you walk together:

- Always obey the traffic guards.

- Cross the street only at the corner.

- Look both ways for cars before crossing the street.

- Walk when crossing the street.

Because young children can see the school bus, they assume the driver can see them. This does not always happen. Most accidents occur in a danger zone that extends ten feet from the bus on all sides. Teach your child to stay five giant steps away from the bus until it is stopped for boarding and never to go back for an item left on the bus or blown under the bus.

Playact riding the school bus with your child, making sure he knows these rules:

- Be on time for the bus.

- Line up single file when getting on the bus.

- Don't push or shove when getting on or off the bus.

- Wait until the bus has stopped completely before boarding.

- Sit down in the seat.

- Talk quietly on the bus.

KINDERGARTEN ENROLLMENT CARD
(Please Print)

199__ - 199__

M ☐
F ☐

Child's Name _____ Preferred Name _____

Date of Birth _____ Place of Birth _____

Birth Certificate No. _____ Home Phone No. _____

Mailing Address _____ City _____ Zip _____

   Subdivision and/or main road nearby _____

Person with whom child lives _____ Relationship to child _____

Father's Name _____ Occupation _____

Father's Place of Employment _____ Phone _____

Mother's Name_____ Occupation _____

Mother's Place of Employment _____ Phone _____

Person to call in an emergency _____ Phone _____

Second choice in an emergency _____ Phone _____

Names and ages of brothers and sisters _____

_____

Previous School Experience: Names of Schools_____

   _____ Address _____

   _____ Dates Attended _____to _____

Child's Special Interests, Talents and Abilities _____

_____

Child has following allergies, disabilities, etc. _____

_____

Please add any other pertinent information about learning problems child

might have _____

_____

Carpool Members: 1. _____ 2. _____

3. _____ 4. _____

MEDICAL HISTORY (Please give dates)

Chicken Pox _____	Polio _____
Whooping Cough _____	Mumps _____
German Measles _____	Measles _____
Pneumonia _____	Scarlet Fever _____
Diphtheria _____	Rheumatic Fever _____
Heart Disease _____	Nephritis _____
Tuberculosis _____	Diabetes _____
Epilepsy _____	Inf. Hepatitis _____
Other Illness _____	
Operations _____	

* *

(Please check)

Frequent Colds _____	Allergy _____
Draining Ears _____	Asthma _____
Convulsions _____	

* *

IMMUNIZATIONS AND TESTS	Dates Month-Day-Year	Boosters
(*Diphtheria	1) _____	
DPT (Pertusis	2) _____	
(*Tetanus	3) _____	
*Polio-Oral	1) _____	
	2) _____	
	3) _____	
*Measles		
*Rubella (3-day Measles)		
*Mumps		
Tuberculin Test		
Others		

Has your child been tested for:	Yes	No
Sickle Cell Anemia	—	—
Lead Poisoning	—	—

Hearing Problems _____

Sight Problems _____

*Immunizations required by state law

117

- Keep head and hands inside the bus.
- Always listen to the bus driver.
- Avoid rowdy play.
- Never chase after the bus.

Be sure to point out that bus drivers need children to be quiet and orderly so they can concentrate on their driving and safely deliver the children to school.

Last Minute Things to Do

Your child is almost ready to start school. His first days at school will be far easier if he feels comfortable in the school environment. If the school does not have an open house, plan a visit to the school with him. Ask at the office the week before school starts for permission for your child to see the areas he will be using. Make sure he can find his classroom and give him a chance to play on the playground equipment.

Even if your child has gone to preschool, he may be apprehensive about kindergarten. Sharing a book such as one of those listed on pages 61–62 will help him feel more comfortable about starting this great new adventure. Playing school with you and his friends will also help your child know what he will be doing in school.

Above All Else

You have prepared your child well for kindergarten during the last five years. Now relax, and let your child see you are confident that he is ready to start school—because you know he is. He has learned about the world with you and his friends in pleasurable ways appropriate for his age. Thanks to your efforts, he brings to kindergarten a love of learning. This, more than anything else, will ensure his success in school in the years to come.

INDEX OF GAMES, SONGS, AND RHYMES

Order Form

Quantity	Title	Author	Order No.	Unit Cost	Total
	Baby & Child Medical Care	Hart, T.	1159	$7.95	
	Baby Name Personality Survey, The	Lansky/Sinrod	1270	$6.95	
	Best Baby Name Book, The	Lansky, B.	1029	$4.95	
	Best Baby Shower, The	Cooke, C.	1239	$5.95	
	Birth Partner's Handbook	Jones, C.	1309	$5.95	
	Dads Say the Dumbest Things!	Lansky, B	4220	$5.95	
	David, We're Pregnant	Johnston, L.	1049	$5.95	
	Discipline w/out Shouting, Spanking	Wyckoff/Unell	1079	$5.95	
	Do They Ever Grow Up?	Johnston, L.	1089	$5.95	
	Feed Me! I'm Yours	Lansky, V.	1109	$7.95	
	First Year Baby Care	Kelly, P.	1119	$6.95	
	Free Stuff for Kids, 1991 Edition	FS Editors	2190	$4.95	
	Getting Organized for Your New Baby	Bard, M.	1229	$4.95	
	Grandma Knows Best	McBride, M.	4009	$4.95	
	Hi Mom! Hi Dad!	Johnston, L.	1139	$5.95	
	Moms Say the Funniest Things!	Lansky, B.	4280	$5.95	
	Mother Murphy's Law	Lansky, B.	1149	$4.50	
	Practical Parenting Tips	Lansky, V.	1179	$6.95	
	Pregnancy, Childbirth, and the Newborn	Simkin/Whalley/Keppler	1169	$10.95	
	Ready for School?	Eberts/Gisler	1360	$5.95	
	Successful Breastfeeding	Price/Dana	1199	$9.95	
	Visualizations for an Easier Childbirth	Jones, C.	1330	$5.95	
	Working Woman's Guide to Breastfeeding	Dana/Price	1259	$6.95	
				Subtotal	
			Shipping and Handling (see below)		
			MN residents add 6% sales tax		
				Total	

YES, please send me the books indicated above. Add $1.25 shipping and handling for the first book and $.50 for each additional book. Add $2.00 to total for books shipped to Canada. Overseas postage will be billed. Allow up to 4 weeks for delivery. Send check or money order payable to Meadowbrook Press. No cash or C.O.D.'s please. Prices subject to change without notice. **Quantity discounts available upon request.**

Send book(s) to:

Name _____

Address _____

City _____ State _____ Zip _____

Phone _____

☐ Check enclosed for $_____ , payable to Meadowbrook Press

☐ Charge to my credit card (for purchases of $10.00 or more only)

Account # _____ ☐ Visa ☐ MasterCard

Signature _____ Expiration date _____

For phone orders call: (800) 338-2232 (for purchases of $10.00 or more only please.)

Write or call for **FREE** catalog.

Meadowbrook Press, 18318 Minnetonka Boulevard, Deephaven, MN 55391
(612) 473-5400   Toll free (800) 338-2232   FAX (612) 475-0736